Safely Taper off Benzodiazepines

A Protocol to Heal Efficiently as Possible and Get Your Life Back

Jenny Karnacewicz (LeslieJ), CHC, M. Ed.

Cover Design: Jennifer Stimson

Editing: Cory Hott

Medical Disclaimer and Liability for Slander

I am not a medical doctor or practitioner. I am a certified health coach with a technical background. None of my suggestions are medical advice. This protocol is simply what I have ascertained to help heal from long-term use of prescribed benzodiazepines. I have used real people's accounts of their experiences about being in benzo hell. All of my information is accurate and not intended to be used as slander or defamation of character. My only goal in including their stories is learn from their experiences.

Contents

This book is dedicated to my mom. Donna Gayle Purdie 11/12/49 to 7/25/22

Please get your carotid arteries checked by ultrasound if you are over fifty and have high cholesterol. My mom was a physically fit, active seventy-two-year-old playing golf with my dad when she died from having a stroke. The statins she took did not prevent cholesterol from blocking her carotid artery and her doctor (seemingly) never checked this in routine exams. There were also no symptoms. I can only find meaning from her death if others learn from this tragedy. But her incredible life will never be unlived as she was an amazing, beautiful person who was dedicated to the value of good health. I love you and miss you, Mom.

My aunt is mentioned often in this book as her support was instrumental to my recovery. She is one of my dad's sisters and her name is Allison Purdie (M. Div., B.S. OTR/L). She wrote the following about my recovery for this book.

> "Jenny gave up everything to forge her way through uncharted territory: benzo withdrawal. Her commitment to this path she would have to develop, and which called into question all of her relationships – even with her well regarded psychiatrist and her entire family.

> "She was no longer any of her labels: mechanical engineer, teacher, mother, and wife. She stood in that place fighting a demon few have taken on – benzo hell. Very slowly she returned to her unmedicated self with the knowledge of how to do it.

> "I am so proud of the survivor she has become."

Chapter 1
Prescribed Dependency

You either picked up this book because you have a feeling that your medication is causing your chronic health issues, or you have already determined that long-term use of benzodiazepines is the source of your suffering. Without this feeling or knowledge, your health would surely continue to deteriorate. I commend your diligence in getting to the bottom of your suffering. I was not as fortunate as you, and neither suspected my medication was the reason for my deteriorating body and mind nor knew what a benzodiazepine was.

The information in this book will bring awareness to what is going on in your body due to the prescribed dependency of benzodiazepines, teach you how to

1

safely taper off this medication and get through this awful withdrawal experience that we call benzo hell. Benzo hell is a syndrome that precipitates, follows and/or coincides with withdrawals from prescribed, long-term use of benzodiazepines. Getting through Benzo Hell will be a journey like no other whether you are just starting to plan your taper or are in Acute withdrawals from cold turkey off the medication. Let this resource help you to get through it so that you make it to the other side where life is even better than it was before this prescription took your mental and physical health away.

Before you continue any further, it is imperative for you to note that abruptly stopping any benzodiazepine can cause acute withdrawals, prolonged suffering, and even have fatal outcomes.

Do not stop this medication abruptly.

The worst possible scenario upon hearing that I was bed ridden and ill from my long-term use and rapid detox from benzos happened when a couple of my (extended) family members, after hearing that I was in such bad shape from this medication, tried to stop their use of long-term prescribed benzodiazepines. One was able to reinstate quick enough to negate the long-term effects of rapid withdrawals but, in my opinion, is still suffering from multiple health conditions that result from long-term use of benzodiazepines.

The other relative I believe is (possibly) permanently damaged as he never gave himself time to heal and has lingering symptoms and conditions of acute withdrawals. Neither of them will allow me to share their stories, but the damage was done. This very unfortunate result was more than enough to convince me that the story that I had to share needed to be about the proper way to get free of this toxic medication. The starting point of finding out your health is failing due to long-term use of benzodiazepines should never be confused with a misguided effort to get off this medication as quick as possible. I am going to try to answer the five most pressing questions that you probably have, but please understand that there is much more to this resource so the rest of the chapters should be read and used to get you through benzo hell.

Is this medication causing my symptoms?

If you are debating whether this medication is causing your health issues, I would like you to answer these two questions.

Do you need to take this medication to feel normal?

And if you try to skip a dose or cut back, do you feel worse?

Ironically, answering yes to these questions proves that the medication is the source of your health issues. It may take a while for you to understand exactly how the dreaded symptoms are proof of a prescribed dependency, but you will get there through my guidance. Until that better understanding is brought forward with further reading, please understand that benzodiazepines are not treating anything but instead are suppressing your reactions to how you are feeling. Even when your muscles are temporarily relaxed or the pain in your jaw dissipates along with the worry about how you were feeling, the "medicine" isn't fixing anything in your body or head. There is no medical benefit to taking these medications long term other than there is an antiseizure (hypnotic) quality for those who are epileptic, but there are far safer options for that purpose. The one and only approved and medically necessary use of benzodiazepines is short-term relief of such distress that the patient may suffer a secondary medical emergency and immediate intervention is required to sedate the patient (most likely in the ER on in extreme grief).

How did this medication get approved by the FDA for long-term use?

The answer is that benzodiazepines are *not* approved for more than ten days of continued use (and even that is pushing the limit as we will find out later). It is a slippery and winding road of marketing deception and research not yet conducted mixed with Big Pharma's ability to smoke screen the timeframe for prescribed use so that doctors can both willingly and unwittingly cause their patients to become dependent on benzodiazepines.

The truth is that none of the following medications were tested and approved to be used more than ten days: Klonopin (Clonazepam), Xanax (Aplrazolam), and Ativan (Lorazepam). All these medications are in the same class as Valium (Diazepam). That is correct. You are taking a medication that everyone knows is only to be used as needed, but the manufacturers rebranded the newer types of benzodiazepines. As a result, we take a much stronger version of Valium daily without even knowing it.

Simply put: the patients are put on the medication leading more drug sales and the doctor prescribes more refills creating more demand. Eventually, the patient begins to "need" the medication to feel normal, and the cycle continues making it appear that benzodiazepines are effective treatments.

I was prescribed both Ativan (as needed) and then daily continuous use of Klonopin without ever knowing that I was taking a medication was in the same class as Valium. I knew that Valium's reputation as "Mother's Little Helper" had caused millions of women in the 1970s to become dependent on a drug which had caused them to become zombies and gave them such rebound anxiety that they were in more distress. Again, it was Big Pharma marketing that successfully rebranded these newer benzodiazepines, even though they work the same way but with different intensities and half-lives.

Why am I now having to take more and different types of medication?

While people are taking the medication and feel progressively worse as tolerance builds (explained in Chapter 4), they then go back to the doctor for other health issues that are simply a result of long-term use of benzodiazepines. And worse, many of them are diagnosed with neurological diseases that the symptoms are mimicking, so they are getting even more medications and treatments leading to even worse conditions. The myriad symptoms that long-term use of benzodiazepines produce is well over 100, and I will list some of them below for your reference. This list was reproduced from the Benzo.org website and curated based on my experience and my clients' experiences. The full list of Symptoms can be found on my website under Resources and is listed as Reference B.

Some common symptoms from prolonged use of benzodiazepines: aggression, anxiety, agoraphobia, apathy, ataxia, breathlessness, chest discomfort and tightness, choking, constipation, convulsions (muscle usually), dental pain, depersonalization, depression, derealization, diarrhea, distortion of body image, misperceptions, dry, itchy skin, "electric shock" feelings throughout the body, dysphoria, head and brain sensations, heart palpitations, hypersensitivity to stimuli, hyperosmia (sensitive sense of smell), hyperpyrexia (overheating), hyperventilation (over-breathing), insomnia, intrusive thoughts, irrational rage, irritability, jumpiness, metallic taste, nausea, nightmares, obsessions, panic attacks, perceptual disturbances and distortions, photosensitivity, psychotic symptoms (usually transient and confined to rapid withdrawal), restlessness, seizures (on abrupt discontinuation), sensory disruption, scalp burning, sore tongue, sweating, night sweats, tinnitus, tremor, vomiting, weakness, "jelly legs," weight gain, weight loss, abnormal muscle tone, aching joints, ataxia, allergic reactions, back pain, blepharospasm (eye twitching), breast pain, apathy, constipation (often alternating with diarrhea), cravings, dehydration, dental pain, dry tickly cough, muscular spasms, muscular (and bone) weakness, myoclonic convulsions (muscle/nerve spasms), nausea, neurological problems (topical nerve anesthesia), nose bleeds, oedema (especially of ankles and face), esophagitis, paranesthesia (numbing, burning and tingling; pins and needles), poor concentration, poor short-term memory, severe headaches, sinusitis, skin insensitivity, sore, itchy eyes, burning sensation in spine, stomach cramps, thirst, thrush-like symptoms, tremor, tinnitus (ear buzzing, anxiety, apnea (night), dyspnea (breathing problems), fatigue, gait disturbance, leaden heaviness, lethargy, libido disturbances, loss of self-confidence, menstrual irregularity, neurological problems, panic attacks, phobias, severe muscle rigidity, short-term memory impairment, vasovagal attacks, vertigo, abnormal behavior or false beliefs, aches and pains (muscle tension),claustrophobia, anger, anti-social behavior, apathy, ataxia, blood disorders (resulting in severe tiredness and possible infections), blurred vision, bradycardia (slow heartbeat/pulse), breast enlargement, changes in appetite chemical sensitivities, allergies, cognitive impairment, confusion, daytime drowsiness, diplopia, dizziness, dry, itchy skin, dysarthria, dysphoria, emotional blunting, exhaustion, fatigue, feeling afraid, feeling unreal, flu-like symptoms, hair loss, hallucinations, hypotension, IBS (Irritable Bowel Syndrome), inability to pass urine/holding of urine in the bladder, impairment of motor co-ordination, incontinence, irritability, jaundice, jaw pains, lack of concentration, lack of confidence, lethargy, many people wonder why they have changed from being happy and outgoing, to being over-anxious and unconfident, memory loss or forgetfulness, mild hypertension, muscle weakness, spasticity, cramps, abnormal tone, nightmares, numbed emotions, panic attacks, personality changes, poor muscle control, problems with vision, psychomotor impairment, rashes, reduced alertness, reduced blood pressure, restlessness, shivering, skin problems, rashes, sleep problems, slurred speech, stomach and bowel problems, stomach upsets, suicidal behavior, thyroid disturbances, and stress intolerance.

While taking benzodiazepines, I was convinced that I was going to die from a fatal heart issue called pulmonary embolism. I had all the symptoms and no doctor could find anything wrong, so I just accepted my pain and fate and gave up trying to fix the problem but lived with a constant doom feeling. I no longer have any heart palpitations, chest constrictions, shortness of breath or fear from dying from this condition which was just a symptom of benzo hell.

In fact, this condition presented when I was in tolerance using Ativan as needed but then was temporarily corrected with the increased benzodiazepine dose and daily use of Klonopin. Then, of course, the symptoms returned with even greater intensity when I was in acute withdrawals.

My point is that if you are on long-term use of prescribed benzodiazepines and have some of the symptoms that are listed, then please understand that more medication (including antidepressants or increased benzodiazepines use) will not fix them long term.

The results from having these symptoms and the person not knowing why they are feeling so terrible is often that they are misdiagnosed with neurological disorders and diseases. Since Big Pharma has no reason to further investigate how this drug creates all these symptoms due to the obvious loss of revenue, there is no real explanation for these symptoms.

This is not a conspiracy theory about doctors wanting to make us sicker. This is about pure lack of evidence-based research and the fact that benzodiazepines do alleviate anxiety related symptoms short term. Many of my clients and benzo warriors who have been diagnosed with such diseases in benzo hell only to have the symptoms reverse on their own by a slow cessation of the benzodiazepines. I am sure that if I had gone to a doctor while experiencing acute symptoms, I would have most certainly been diagnosed with Parkinson's disease due to my uncontrollable tremors and constant shaking. Here is a shortened list of misdiagnosed illnesses that I obtained from by Benzo Information Coalition on their website. It is listed as Reference C on my website.

Common misdiagnosed illness from long term use of prescribed benzodiazepines: Hashimoto's disease, lupus, Lyme disease, rheumatoid arthritis, hypertension or hypotension, postural orthostatic tachycardia syndrome (POTS), tachycardia, dental cavities, dry mouth, tooth pain, Cushing's disease, hypoglycemia, hyperthyroidism, hypothyroidism, insulin resistance, acid reflux, gastritis, irritable bowel syndrome, Ehlers-Danlos, cancer, interstitial cystitis, mast cell activation syndrome (MCAS), recurrent infections, amyotrophic lateral sclerosis (ALS), confusion, fibromyalgia, migraines, multiple sclerosis, muscle weakness, myalgic encephalomyelitis (Chronic Fatigue Syndrome), neuralgia, neuropathy, numbness, Stiff-Person Syndrome, tinnitus, vertigo, blurred vision, dry eyes, bipolar disorder, borderline personality disorder, conversion disorder, catatonia, depression, dementia, dissociative disorders, generalized anxiety disorder, insomnia, mania, Obsessive-Compulsive Disorder, panic disorder with or without agoraphobia, paranoia, psychosis, PTSD, self-harm, Somatoform Disorder, erectile dysfunction, infertility, irregular menstruation, and polycystic ovary syndrome.

Paraphrasing from the Benzo Information Coalition (BIC) website: the patient goes to the doctor and often gets short-term relief from a minor (non-life threatening) health issue by getting a prescription for a benzodiazepine and then develops chronic secondary health issues from long-term use of that same prescription. A new medical issue which arises from a medical intervention is called an iatrogenic injury. The last chapter of this book lists and refers to other sources of those types of initial health concerns or conditions. My story is a bit different as you will read because the daily use of Klonopin was indeed addressing what I thought was a life-threatening condition, but it was in fact simply inter-dose withdrawal from using prescribed Ativan as needed. A direct quote from the BIC website summarizes this perfectly. "Were the benzodiazepine identified and then removed in a safe manner via slow taper, nearly all the mysterious symptoms and conditions would slowly resolve on their own." Please Reference C in my Resources on my Website.

Will I heal?

This story is being written by you as I healed in my story. There is a ton of regret, grief, anger, and remorse when we find out that we caused our compromised health by taking this prescribed medication. I am a degreed engineer who prided myself on getting to the bottom of things with "mad-dog," like effort in learning and applying electro-mechanical applications. This little, tiny pill took my life away, and it was done without me even being told that Klonopin was a benzodiazepine like Xanax. (I think I had at least heard of Xanax before.)

I let that happen, and now, I am rewriting my story to have an even better life after years of debilitating symptoms and feeling ill.

However, I need to make this clear: it is a process and not a product that I am going to teach through this iterative protocol of healing. You are going to recover from the damage of long-term use of benzodiazepines and be healthy, happy again. And hopefully like me, you will find out there is so much more to life than you ever knew before this withdrawal process. But you are not going to ask yourself "when will I be healed" and just look at that projected date as whether you succeed or not. I am not able to definitively say when you will heal, but I will guide you to the best way for you to heal as efficiently as possible from my experience and that of many other benzo warriors. A benzo warrior identifies someone who not only survived but flourished with this iatrogenic injury.

How did I let this happen to me?

Finally, let's return to how benzodiazepines did help us feel better short-term to identify how we let this happen to us. We relied on doctors and their professional practice to help with a health concern that was ailing us. In my case, it was a racing heart and a stressful work situation. I took my first

Klonopin at around noon, and all my symptoms disappeared by 1:00 p.m. I told my doctor that it was a miracle drug. (By the way, she would remind me of this statement almost a year after my rapid detox and my response was, "I bet if you had given me cocaine then I would have felt that was a miracle drug too.")

That first dose was in fact just masking the inter-dose withdrawals (to be explained further later) and tolerance of the as-needed Ativan that I had been taking for ten years. After learning how benzos were discovered, you will understand how this utterly disappointing failure by supposed medical experts could have happened.

A medical chemist named Leo Sturnbach (born in 1908) was working on developing a pharmaceutical that would be a safer anti-anxiety drug than the older class of benzodiazepines called barbiturates (one could quite easily over-dose on barbiturates due to how they work) by experimenting with mice. A byproduct of one of his chemical compounds crystalized, and by complete and utter happenstance, he administered to them with highly effective results. He wasn't an evil person with a hidden agenda but rather a well-educated chemist who thought he had done a great service as told in his obituary. He is even on record confirming the answer to the first question with the quote:

"It had no unpleasant side effects. It gives you the feeling of well-being. Only when the sales figures came in, I realized how important it was."

Economics, not true efficacy of medical viability drove the success of benzodiazepines to become the most profitable mediation in the world. But even then, when the medication was released to the public it was not recommended to be used for more than two weeks.

What happened in his testing lab with mice will further explain how we were literally "duped" into believing in the efficacy of this drug. The mice were administered the benzodiazepine and then placed in a cage that had a tilting screen in the bottom. After they were sedated, the screen was tilted to a steep angle. The mice rolled down the screen into a pile at the lowest point. They did not fight to regain stability by climbing back up the screen but were in fact quite content to be piled on top of each other. These mice showed no clinical signs of anxiety, and the compound was deemed a successful anti-anxiety medication.

This is what benzos do to humans and over longer periods of usage time. They no longer notice when their health (brain and body) becomes fully compromised. We were so pleased with whatever ailment (most likely anxiety and panic but other states too) that we happily, without knowing the consequences, took the medication as prescribed. And we kept taking it as the doctor refilled the prescription.

Until now.

It is time to take your health back.

Chapter 2

My Story Getting into Benzo Hell

As I am writing this, it has been almost four years to the day when I jumped off 1 mg of Klonopin, which I had been prescribed to take daily for three and a half years. Three days ago, I started playing in a competitive golf league and had so much fun socializing and being part of a team sport again. I had to rest a bit more the following day. Then I went grocery shopping, did laundry, and cleaned the bathrooms without any anxiety or pain. I walk my dog daily and enjoy many activities outside. I often cook family dinners and delight in being able to do it as well as finding new recipes to try. I am going to a high school baseball game tonight.

I am telling you all this so that when you read my story, you will understand just how far I have come. I am not sharing my story to be triumphant. My story is going to show you how healing is possible, and that the definition of healing isn't getting the life you had before benzos back. It is a known fact that part of this journey is thinking that you are the worst-case scenario and will never heal. I am here to say otherwise with my story.

It started with the use of Ativan (Lorazepam is the generic) as needed after the birth of my daughter. At least, I thought it did until I dug deeper. I had severe postpartum depression and was given many drugs to deal with debilitating fatigue, racing anxiety, constant body tremors, muscle aches, and the inability to care for her or myself. Seventeen years later, after I quit the benzos, these symptoms raged back to the nth degree, and these horrible symptoms were added: impaired cognition, extreme muscle and bone pain, loss of fine motor skills, unable to feel extremities, derealization, depersonalization where I felt I was another being trapped in a body, something called air-hunger (if you never had it then be grateful), and many more mental and physical tortures.

What I finally put together after many months of research and reflecting was that I was given a sedative called Versa (a benzodiazepine) during my labor at the hospital. I had gone into labor at midnight. Apparently, arriving at that time wasn't convenient for the hospital staff or the on-call doctor (who didn't arrive until 7:00 a.m. that following morning), so they wanted to keep me calm and inactive for the night. I was given two doses, and by the time my real doctor showed up, I was too sedated to push nor did I want to.

My daughter was born at noon the next day without a cry as she was also sedated with a low APGAR rating. Depleted from the long labor and the benzodiazepine, I was thrown into a panic that sparked my symptoms when I returned home from the hospital, which was essentially withdrawals. But the continued use of Ativan as needed over the following years (all while still drinking socially) lead to the increased need for more medication. I did not know any of this was happening nor had I been informed that alcohol essentially kindles the negative effects of the sedative (further down regulates the same GABA receptors as it acts like a liquid benzo). I

21

started my dream career that I worked three years to obtain when I experienced something so profound that I again sought medical help. I was told that the Ativan wasn't strong enough and that I needed to be on a daily dose of Klonopin. That was more than seven years ago.

I decided to make a career change from being an applications engineer to middle school math teacher as I approached being forty years old. I threw myself into the certification process, student teaching, being a para-professional, and then getting a master's in STEM education. This career change took three years while being a mom to our then elementary school age kids and a wife to my self-employed husband. It was a lot. But my desire to contribute to the next generation's education in a way that would make a difference drove me to succeed at all costs, which was setting me up for needing more medication for my health. I was also playing competitive tennis and doing as much as I could to keep up with family activities. I loved the new Common Core standards and felt like I was going to be part of a huge turn-around in our country's technical abilities as students would learn the value of applying math concepts instead of memorizing the procedures. So, when I finally got my first teaching position as a sixth grade math teacher, I was beyond ecstatic with anticipation of a rewarding career as well as to be able to provide health insurance for my family.

Worst Decision of My Life

When I was offered my position at a middle school, I was told that we as teachers are often asked to take on more roles than the classroom teacher in order to be part of the school's staff. I played and coached soccer basically all my life, so I accepted the middle school girls' soccer coaching position, which of course started right when school began in the fall. If you can see disaster coming from what I have explained thus far, then you will learn that I was in over my head from the start. The teachers at this school were less than supportive of me due to the conditions under which I was hired. There was a new testing protocol called Performance Testing being test-run by the school, and the consulting point person for this testing recommended me for the job as someone who would be supportive of this program. The principal did not consult the other faculty, and I showed up the first day to a team of teachers grudgingly accepting me as the new teacher. Although I had excellent para-professional support, I was criticized for the classroom management style that I had learned would be most effective for group participation.

I was now taking 0.5 mg Ativan almost daily to cope with the stress of the long hours and frequent administrative duties that were becoming the priority of my classroom's agenda. I was a mess and not even remotely eating or resting adequately. I left daily with headaches that were becoming worse due to tolerance of Ativan and then my heart started flipping out. Literally. I sought medical help and was told nothing was wrong. So, I ended up in a psychiatrist's office and was told that Ativan wasn't sufficient for my "anxiety" and that I needed daily 1mg of Klonopin (which I filled as the generic Clonazepam).

At first, this drug was like a miracle. It worked to take away the racing heart, the weak-kneed anxiety, and body tremors. It even helped with my muscle stiffness. That is not surprising now as I understand that Klonopin is also a muscle relaxant. I can honestly say that I was "good to go" for about five months in which I taught middle school math, coached the girls' soccer team, and kept up with my family's activities. Then life began to openly disintegrate along with my mental and physical health.

Memory and tendons were all but failing. My time was divided between being upright to accomplish what I needed to (while enjoying nothing) and laying down to rest. I thought it was the teaching job, which proved to be far more demanding than my engineering positions. I thought it was family stress. I thought it was my body aging. I never thought it was the benzodiazepines, a class of drugs approved only for short-term use (maximum of two weeks) prescribed for as many in one in five people under the names of Xanax (Alprazolam), Ativan (Lorazepam), Klonopin (Clonazepam), and Valium (Diazepam).

I didn't even know that the drug I was taking was in the same category as Valium. And this is not an uneducated person. I simply trusted my doctor and took this poison for three and a half years while my life fell apart, and I chased the individual symptoms by paying many doctors, rushing to ER visits, having surgery for my Achilles tendon, and adding alcohol to deal with the paradoxical effects of using Klonopin long term. To say that I also put my family through Hell is probably an understatement in that the raging that I did during this time was completely insane. All of these symptoms and more can be found at a useful and life-saving site called BenzoBuddies.org. It is stupefying that doctors still prescribe this medication after the thousands of anecdotal evidence found on this website alone. Google benzo withdrawals and many more YouTube videos and testaments will be easily found. This is not new information. And this problem of epidemic prescribed benzo use is getting worse, not better.

It was my husband, not a doctor, who finally pulled the plug on this medication induced craziness. I was battling with him daily over the behavior of our son. Our son is a kind, sensitive boy who had obedience issues starting from age two. However, his defiance escalated into school and sports and was affecting our daughter. I thought he had to go away for residential treatment. My husband said I needed to get off the benzos. I did not think these two issues were remotely related other than the Klonopin helped me relax for shorter and shorter periods of time as I grew tolerant of the medication. But I decided to prove him wrong and went away to a remote location (our ski house in Maine) to rapidly detox off the benzos. My husband checked with my doctor about this decision, and it was approved due to the "low dosage" that I was taking.

Second Worst Mistake of My Life

This was the second worst mistake of my life on June 4, 2018 – second to not researching benzos when it was prescribed by a doctor. As Stevie Nicks from Fleetwood Mac states perfectly of her rapid detox of Klonopin in 1994 (why hadn't I heard about this before?) "The gates of Hell opened up," and this is what happened from as much as I can remember.

I had exactly enough 0.5 mg of Klonopin pills to do a ten-day detox of reducing each day by a quarter of a pill. With absolute foolishness, I had decided to do this type of detox based on what I had seen online with advertisements from facilities offering such types of detoxes.

I lined up the pills with the reduction for each day on the windowsill and went from there. The symptoms of tolerance were already bad with headaches, deep pain ear pressure, and muscle aches, but the first cut doubled that pain by the second day.

By the third day, I was living in complete derealization (everything appeared fake), and I was no longer able to walk my dog. I was checking in with my aunt daily, and she advised me to get some food delivered, which was another one of the many things that I could not have planned on my own but ended up probably saving my life. I was barely able to speak coherently, but I called a local grocer and told the man that I was sick and needed prepared food to be delivered. This is a small community in Maine at Sunday River, and I was grateful that he understood and ended up bringing food for the next week and leaving it at my door. I did get a literal "taste" of what was to come though as I remember thinking that food never tasted so good as I was getting my taste buds back after not knowing they were dampened by the benzodiazepines for years.

I entered the phase of terror on the fifth day and feared everything. I could not do any laundry as it was too exhausting to walk down the stairs. I was so weak that I could not open or lift the dog food, so I cut a hole in it and let my dog get her own food. I stopped sleeping and felt like I was being electrocuted. My bone aches were going to get a lot worse, but I had started shaking when I stood with what is referred to as "jelly legs".

By the sixth day, I was hallucinating and not recognizing myself in the mirror. All my muscles were stiff, and I could not fathom moving without a clear plan for effort. There was an owl about the size of my dog watching me from the side of my view and would flap its wings when I would lose consciousness. This could not get worse until it did.

I had not showered and was now afraid of the bathwater, so I decided that I would try to use a face cloth to clean myself. This is the last real memory I have but would find out more bizarre things that happened upon my return to that house months later.

I remember not being able to move my arms in a coordinated fashion to clean myself and that everything was in slow motion. It was like I was underwater. It was two more days before my husband drove up to bring me home. I had called him with panic that my head was going to explode and recall that he was dealing with my son (who was twelve at the time) and some behavioral issue. I know that I had got into the melatonin and the Benadryl medications, and maybe I had taken so much of it that I was sedated during this time, but I do know that I felt like I was being tortured alive and had little awareness of what was real or not.

I had stopped on the way to my ski house to get some food, staples that included Gatorade Propel which to this day I think also saved my life. No one knows what is happening in acute withdrawals, but we do become extremely deficient in some minerals and vitamins, and I believe that the Gatorade Propel sustained me although I have no proof at all.

Also, these Gatorade bottles had the plastic and pop lids instead of the screw caps, so I was able to open them. In addition to having my dog for company and being a constant source of companionship over the next few years, I felt another presence with that hallucinated owl and will never know if a higher power was there to save me. I am not religious, so I can't explain it. I had ice on my head constantly and also used it on my back, but other than that, I simply suffered and waited. It was so unbelievably dumb of me to do this, but I think once I was past the point of no return knowing that my doctor canceled my prescription once she was told that I was detoxing, I felt compelled to finish and did exactly that. I barely survived and was brought home by my husband to be bed-ridden for the next two to three months.

Figuring Things Out

When I got home, I was confused about what was going on and why it was happening, but I managed to get on the computer. I was not able to sit up for long and my hands would get numb, but I did find a Brian Baxter YouTube video (Reference J Benzo Withdrawal Welcome to Full Hell2 under Resources on my website) on this experience and finally understood (not in its entirety) that I was in acute withdrawals, and it would be a long healing process. But just by learning this and having someone validate my symptoms, I immediately stopped feeling like I was going crazy and doubting if I was going to survive, even though things would get worse before they got better.

On the third day that I was home the cortisol rushes started in the early morning, and I bolted out of bed in such fright that I knew I was dying. I wanted to call 911, but my husband put in a call to the psychiatrist who had both prescribed this medication and said that a ten-day detox off such a low dose was fine to do. This doctor called back to tell us that I needed to see her for more medication as my anxiety was causing this panic attack. Had I not known that this rebound anxiety (which was far worse anxiety than I ever had in my life) was due to withdrawals, then I probably would now be on even more sedating medication or quite frankly not be alive right now. I knew I was on my own from then on out.

I will be explaining what I did for all my symptoms as I got through benzo hell, but this is my story as I was experiencing it. Within the next two days, I was immobilized with joint pain and muscle stiffness. My neck was so weak that I could not lift my head. My husband called her back for the last time, and she said that I was probably just getting weak from lying in bed. I am an athlete with much training. It was the most condescending thing I was ever told, even though I would experience muscle wasting later on in this recovery, but I was certainly not there yet.

My skin dried up and my hair turned gray – all of my hair, everywhere. I was peeing every ten to fifteen minutes. My hair was an oily mess even if I had the strength to wash it as my scalp was releasing peptides. The deep fatigue took my breath away when standing. My legs were like jelly and my hands swollen with inflammation. I could not get enough air into my lungs and was thinking that I was suffocating.

Then the jerking started. My limbs would flail for no reason or if I was even slightly touched. I could not see much even with my glasses on. I was scared to even look outside and had to hide from any stimulation to my senses. There is a cartoon that depicts us in acute benzo withdrawals that shows a person being hooked up to a car battery, and that is exactly how I felt. I was being electrocuted from the inside with both bolts that would take my breath away and a surface electrification on my skin. I could not stand the touch of any fabric other than cotton. Any noises or smells put me into a complete rage. Now, I just wanted to die and often thought of ways of doing it.

Brain Injury Diagnosed

At about two weeks after I got home, I had a glimpse of feeling a little bit better and went down to the kitchen to help with the dishes. My husband was taking the primary role in all the house stuff, but my daughter (who was fourteen) was also doing a lot of my chores. I just wanted to help. There was a pile of dishes in the sink, but the dishwasher was full of clean dishes as indicated by the green light. I stared at the dishwasher for many minutes without the ability to figure out what to do first. I knew what I had to do. I had some energy to do it. I just could not figure out what to do.

I went back to my room and called my aunt, who is an occupational therapist and loves me very much. She asked me a few questions to which I answered yes, including a pulling down sensation of my head. With a few more diagnostics, she calmly explained that I had a brain injury and that she would help me to heal. It would take time, but she knew what I had to do and that included resting without judgement right now. I will detail her protocol in the rest of the book, but that was how I survived and wanted to keep going. With her daily encouragement, I slowly got better – and you will too.

About six weeks after I got home from the detox, both of my children left on separate trips that were planned for the summer. It was another divine intervention. I started stuttering and was in bad mental and physical shape that I could not hide from them. They were gone for about ten days.

This is a critical part of my recovery as I had developed agoraphobia by this point and had been unable to leave the house. I started my exposure therapy with my aunt at this time, and it needed to be done without stress. My daughter planted a garden in the cul de sac of our neighborhood that included an abundance of kale. I never ate kale before this. But it was my daily venture to get past the mailbox and sit in that garden and eat her vegetables; this was the beginning of healing for me.

You have the resources to heal even if you don't know it. Finding a sanctuary in my daughter's garden didn't just happen to me; it was planted for a reason. Others experienced similar findings in their environments when they were curious and willing enough to start (very slowly) taking their life back from this iatrogenic injury.

Where I am today, helping people to find out if their medication is causing their chronic illness and then supporting them as they deal with benzo hell, is a far cry from where I was in benzo hell. I came to a pivotal place in my healing when I entered the recovery stage. How I define this stage is when you are no longer just trying to survive as opposed to being in acute, when your only thoughts are about how to get through the minute, hour, and day.

I would have got to this stage in time, but I had the professional help of my aunt who I am now trying to emulate with my coaching. She held the belief that I would not only survive but be better than I was by going through this process. I now do that for other people. I make sure they covet their recovery state by protecting their small improvements while advancing what they can do functionally. My aunt's unique qualifications for guiding me to become a functional benzo warrior with the capacity to help others include being an occupational therapist, an ordained minister, a person who experienced traumatic brain injury herself, and an innate ability to sense when people need to be pushed or to rest. As her story has become part of my story, I want my story to inspire and become your story.

I walk without pain and think clearly. I still limit myself in some activities in either duration or intensity but have no regrets doing this. Learn from me as I did and do from her.

Chapter 3

Framework for Using This Resource and Expectations from Implementing the Protocol

Moving the Needle

The primary use of this book is to state that there is no cure or antidote for what has been damaged by long-term use of benzodiazepines but rather to understand that there are ways to optimize healing through lifestyle choices. There is a term that I learned in my health coaching certification called "moving the needle." For those of the newer digital generation, the term should be explained as I am not sure they have even seen or experienced analog gauges or meters. These are devices that detect something such as sound (vibration) or concentration of a particle (ex: radio-active material) in a measurable way from zero to the max. You may have seen old war movies where the signal was found on such a contraption and the needle moved just slightly but enough for either celebration or peril. Business then adopted that term, and now, the health industry has, too, as it means getting a positive reaction from stimuli.

The goal in this protocol is to "move the needle" just as slightly as possible in the right direction of healing as we get relief from our symptoms. But the gauge in this context of this protocol is not measuring how much our symptoms are resolving but rather our ability to self-regulate our nervous system. Anything that pegs the needle to max will be either detrimental to long-term healing (a temporary effect) or will not be sustainable during recovery. We will discuss this more with each addressed symptom but the important concept to fully recognize before progressing to the protocol is that we are going through a process and not trying to achieve an end product.

Getting through benzo hell requires taking iterative steps forward and backwards to heal, and that was the most difficult part for me and others to accept.

The reason that I am encouraging you to focus on that process and not the product of healing is strangely surreal. Having the intention of healing while moving the needle is how this protocol works. This is mutually exclusive from the focus of healing to be looking for resulting improvements that will keep you judging as that state is not conducive to healing. Be assured that healing is happening because of you using this protocol.

Nonlinear Healing

Perhaps an even more maddening part of this process of healing is that it is not a straight line from the injury to healing when tracking recovery. I chose to track the intensity of the symptoms decreasing as I healed which means that the graph my trends down to recovery instead of up. I am attempting to show you that my months in the recovery stage were made up of drastic changes in the intensity of these symptoms but it is almost impossible to show how even these changed within days as well (due to the resolution of the illustration). The yellow arrow is depicting the decrease of symptoms over time.

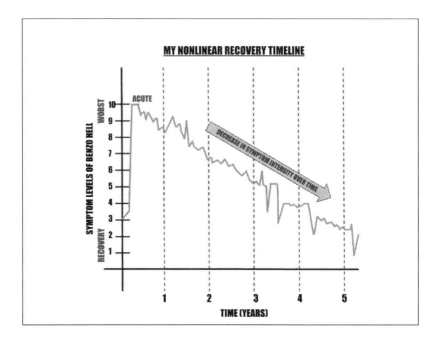

Windows and Waves and Baseline

There are terms that define this nonlinear process of healing that are use called baseline, windows, and waves.

A window is when the debilitating symptom lessens or disappears for brief (not permanent) periods of time.

A wave is when that symptom comes back and sometimes even more intensely.

The baseline is how we are consistently feeling and is indicated with the horizontal runs on the graph (which isn't shown again due to the resolution). When working with other benzo warriors who have experience in tracking their recovery (which is not necessary but is used to remind of us progress as well will get to), it is often declared that our baseline increases after a wave. My experience has verified this as well. I will get into the stages of benzo hell in the next section, but it is important to understand that waves and windows occur within these stages and are not only indicative of how something is affecting your recovery (any stimulation) but are also just part of the healing process.

My aunt was able to verify this nonlinear healing phenomenon as she has worked with brain trauma patients who would display this same type of forward and backward healing during their recovery. The increasing and then decreasing symptoms are a re-affirming characteristic of this injury that shows we are not permanently damaged but have an impairment that is healing.

While the majority will have this nonlinear recovery with windows and waves, there are some who do not have these windows and waves but still go on to heal in a much more subtle way. In either of these ways of healing, the premise for the protocol is that if we are aware of our states and what has helped or made them worse, then we are better at reproducing or avoiding them. That is what I am going to teach you (or reinforce this instinctive habit) to do with your recovery. I would like to encourage you to read this book from beginning to end and then use what you need to reference as it applies to you. Reading about what could happen and how to deal with it is like knowing what to expect instead of being blindsided and start chasing the symptoms.

Stages of Benzo Hell

The stages of benzo hell include tolerance, inter-dose withdrawal, paradoxical, acute, recovery, setbacks, protracted, and enlightened. No one has to go through every stage to get through benzo hell, and one stage is not necessary for the next stage to happen. It is just a way of labeling where you are on this path so that care is taken at the appropriate steps to start or continue healing. Some of my clients will oscillate between acute and recovery and get frustrated as I sure did in my journey, but that is what this injury is – a transient state as our nervous system re-regulates. Do not get discouraged as I am going to make sure you understand what can be done to stabilize even in the setback stage.

Tolerance

You are in tolerance when the benzodiazepine is no longer working to suppress your nervous system and other health related maladies begin to appear. I have worked with people who have developed tolerance quickly, and for others, it took years to happen.

One client took benzodiazepines for almost a decade at the same dose without having symptoms of tolerance until they stopped their daily alcohol drinking habit. A few other clients developed tolerance within weeks of taking a daily dose. The biggest problem with tolerance is that many people's benzodiazepine prescription dose gets increased during this time as the doctor simply doesn't recognize that the patient is experiencing an increased need for more sedation due to dependency and not outside circumstances. It would be quite useful to simply ask the patient what has changed to cause the need for increased anxiety to determine this, but instead, more medication is prescribed to mask the symptoms of tolerance. It is truly a tragedy that extends the recovery when the patient finally decides to get off the benzodiazepines.

Interdose Withdrawals

Interdose withdrawals was my first sign that I was in trouble with my daily use of Klonopin. My years of interdose withdrawals on 0.5mg of Klonopin twice a day went like this.

I would wake up (usually damp from sweating while sleeping) and immediately feel a surge of anxiousness. Ten minutes after taking my first dose, I would be calm enough to prioritize what I had to get done in the day before the anxiousness returned as well as other uncomfortable symptoms. Why I never once questioned this daily sequence to be related to the medication will be addressed, but back then, I simply thought that it was proving that I needed benzodiazepines. I would rush around and get as much done without enjoying anything until about 2:30 (yes, it was like clockwork) and then my increased symptoms of withdrawals would start. I would then take my second dose and crash into bed, feeling I had done enough for the day with the exception of getting up to make dinner. Meanwhile, I was going to doctors chasing my ever-increasing symptoms of GI issues, heart palpitations, more and more fatigue, skin issues, and the dreaded achilles tendons break-down, which I will go into further in Chapter 5.

Paradoxical

Padoxical reaction to a medication means that there is an immediate negative affect to taking it. I have had paradoxical reactions to medications but not to benzodiazepines. That experience of negatively reacting to medication leaves me wondering how anyone could continue to take their medication if there are negative side effects. But I have found that there are indeed people who have been on prescribed long-term use of benzodiazepines who had immediate paradoxical reactions and continued to take these medications. These negative side effects do seem to dissipate quicky after stopping the benzo.

However, what I want you to know about the paradoxical stage in benzo hell is that it can happen when a person is either up-dosing or reinstating their use of benzodiazepines. This is significant information regarding recovery as I am highly encouraging you to avoid doing either one of these things and thereby entering the paradoxical stage. I know that it is difficult to hear this if you have already either up-dosed or reinstated, but this is being stated for the others who are reading this and learning to be proactive in their recovery. I would have not known this either, and as more of my story unfolds, you will see that I could have easily entered the paradoxical stage myself.

Acute

The acute withdrawal part of injury usually occurs when the drug is taken away abruptly, and the person is just about surviving each day as I documented in Chapter 2 with my story. Acute withdrawal usually happens after abrupt cessation (rapid detox) of the drug and can also occur with a taper if the reductions are too large and the person was on the medications for years. But much to my dismay and horror of some short-term users, it is shown that just three weeks of consistent use of benzodiazepines can lead to acute as well.

Protracted

The protracted stage is the term used for symptoms of withdrawals lasting more than eighteen months (as defined by BenzoBuddies.org). The protracted stage could have periods of acute-like symptoms (as I had) or could just be waves and windows as the person progresses in recovery. What is important to do in the protracted stage is recognize you are not going to be like this forever, but your body needs some extra time and encouragement to heal. The caveat about the protracted stage is that is easy to forget that your baseline is improving while dealing with the daily ups and downs of the intensity of symptoms. I remind clients (as my aunt reminded me) about symptoms that disappeared as the focus seems to remain on ongoing or sometimes new symptoms.

Recovery

What I am going to primarily concentrate on in this protocol is the recovery stage of the person properly tapering off the medication or after having been in the acute stage for others like me. I call this the recovery stage as it is a both critical and pivotal opportunity in time to heal and should be protected at all costs to prevent chronic illnesses. Again, I was lucky to have my aunt by my side during this stage as I would have surely blown it more than I already did when I was feeling better. This stage is the hardest for people who think that recovery means being able to do more. The point of recovery is to ensure that you will be able to do what you are doing again and again and then to capitalize on how your body re-regulates after the activity. It is not about pushing yourself past limits as what is done when training for sports. The recovery stage is about allowing the body to synthesize the productivity gains and to encourage the brain to start re-mapping the response to stimuli.

Origins of This Protocol

As I have already stated, most, if not all, of what I am going to share in this book (healing protocol) has been learned from others and curated by me to help support you. There is nothing new or novel about these strategies in health coaching except that they are modified to address our symptoms in benzo hell. What traditional services and therapy advise and suggest for matters of general health usually don't apply to our situations in the acute and recovery stages of benzo hell. A good representable example is reviewing traditional recommendations for insomnia, which includes sleep deprivation until the allotted time to develop a schedule. This is not conducive to our situation where rest is elusive, so instead of focusing on regulating our circadian rhythms, we need to prioritize getting that coveted sleep whenever possible. The matter of obtaining that restful state for short periods of time is what the protocol addresses and not how to schedule long slumbers just at night.

Much of what I am going to share is how my aunt was able to provide me with the knowledge on when to start actively "moving the needle" based on the reassessment of the baseline progressing forward. There is no timeline with benzo recovery as every person enters this with different DNA, history of use, resources to heal (all you), and available support. But with this resource, you will heal as efficiently as possible and hopefully avoid the worst stage of recovery called setbacks. A setback is when progress is wiped out or severely regressed due to either a supplement, an overstimulating event, an avoidable medical intervention*, chronic stress from fighting the injury, a negative life altering event, a toxic chemical, or an unknown deterrent that we have yet to identify.

*Some medical interventions are necessary due to pre-existing conditions and thus cannot be avoided.

The Members of Our Community as Part of the Protocol

Getting through benzo hell is a scary and lonely process. I encourage anyone either preparing for this or in it to lean on others who went through it. We call these people benzo warriors. The problem is that there are few of us willing to share after we have made our recoveries due to obvious reasons. We are living our lives. We are also reluctant to remember the tortuous weeks, months, and even years and, therefore, would rather forget that they ever happened. When I found BenzoBuddies.org which is an online forum giving peer support, I was super excited to converse with others in my situation and have my symptoms validated. I admit that I would spend hours on this website giving support daily for months while getting tidbits of information that would help my symptoms. But it turned into a bad habit for me as I progressed out of acute and into recovery as I was almost obsessed with trying to help others. I learned a ton and started being prescriptive in giving advice which was immediately shut down by the administrators. It is hard to understand how a worldwide resource, BenzoBuddies.org, wouldn't appreciate learning from other benzo warriors, but I eventually accepted that this forum was for validation only. They have gone on to add a linked survey that is being done to get the FDA to address the damage caused by long-term benzodiazepine use, so they are being part of the solution with this feature.

Being estranged from BenzoBuddies.org is what propelled me to become a benzo recovery health coach as I wanted to do something more than say, "Yeah, I had that too." I wanted to offer suggestions without being shut down. I did not need or want yet another career but instead felt compelled to further my education on how to help others with health issues specifically resulting from long-term use of benzodiazepines. I began a six-month program to become a certified health coach when I was no longer in acute and could handle such schooling.

I am now committed to helping others through benzo hell while maintaining and furthering my health recovery as my priority. This is not an easy feat at all due to the despairing state of suffering that we are in during benzo hell. We are fighting for our lives and may be eager to try anything as well as answer-shop to find solutions. And when we find something that works for us, we want the whole community to know about it.

But having just one person with either a reaction or a possible fluke in their healing that they think was related to something external is dangerous for the rest of us. None of us are experts on anything but ourselves in benzo hell unless there is some sort of clinical research that I have yet to find out about. We do have awesome benzo warriors sharing information, like Don Killian who suffered a significant setback from overdoing it with binaural beats. I am so grateful for what I have learned and applied from others while also being guilty of attacking someone for not agreeing with my assessments due to my volatile state of distress. My point is that this protocol is evolving based on statistical data coming in from the community. What I am putting in this resource is what I have found to be true by working with people directly as well as reading their stories and following their journeys through benzo hell. I continue to be to up to date on reading the available information online from reputable sources and share them with you.

Dream Come True

My dream would be to have medical support for this iatrogenic injury normalized by our healthcare system. A benzo warrior made a video to show what that would look like, and although it is simply a rendition of what we would like to see happen, it is truly what we need. Please see Reference H on my website for the video made by BenzoLand. How many are now suffering and unable to work due to being in benzo hell and don't even know what the true cause is? This lack of awareness leads to people making themselves worse by not healing but rather making their health worse. It is my belief that a ton of people who are now on government supported disability have been harmed by these medications and just don't know it. Or even worse, they may now know how badly they are off and why but don't have a correct medical diagnosis with all the necessary accommodations that she is providing in her video to do something to heal themselves. Rather than lament on this absolute shit storm of epic proportions, I am here to help you to recover the best way possible. We are not going around, under, or over benzo hell with this protocol but through it to come out a stronger, healthier person who owns their health rather than let an uninformed or misguided doctor ruin it.

Chapter 4

Technical Explanation for What Is Going On in Benzo Hell

Benzodiazepines are a class of medication named for the molecular structure which includes the bonding of the benzine to the diazepine ring. They work by binding to the specific sites on the GABA neuroreceptors site that enhance chloride ions flow to increase the calming affect on the central nervous system. The inhibitory effects of the medication are real and not a placebo effect. There are more than a dozen types of benzodiazepines, but they all work in the same way in that they cross the blood-brain barrier and change the function of neuroreceptors and eventually the neurotransmitters.

Neuroreceptors and neurotransmitters are responsible for cell-to-cell communication and, when altered by artificial means, interrupt the ability of them to regulate homeostasis in our cells. These medications produce a calming effect by specifically bonding to the GABA A receptor which produces a higher potential controlling the inhibition between transmitter and receptor. We already learned that Valium (Diazepam) was the most popular benzodiazepine until it was discovered to be addictive, (which was really dependency) and thus, the other popular brands were generated in a marketing scheme.

Different Types of Benzodiazepines

The main difference in these types of benzodiazepines is their ability to penetrate through the blood-brain barrier at different rates and concentrations. A complete list of benzodiazepines can be found on the DEA drug fact sheet that is listed as Reference K on my website. The irony that this book is about a prescribed dependency and yet the best, most concise information comes from the DEA isn't lost on me nor should be for you. Benzodiazepines, unlike opiates, do not produce a "high," so why would they be sought out and abused?

The answer is that the calming effects of long-term use are not medicinal (not curing) but create more need for more of the drug. We are not addicts as discussed in Chapter 1 but were prescribed a medication that essentially made us part of a larger problem that we shouldn't ignore. Self-medicating with illicit drugs was never part of my story and probably not yours, but this is yet another indication of just how dangerous of a medication we are dealing with.

PsychDB is a free psychiatry reference for medical students, residents and physicians and stated the following: "Benzodiazepines are a class of psychotropic medications with sedative-hypnotic, anxiolytic, anticonvulsant, and muscle relaxant effects. Benzodiazepines are among the most misused and misprescribed medications in the world. Benzodiazepines carry a risk of increased sedation, cognitive impairment, and respiratory depression in those with liver impairments, and there is an increased risk of respiratory depression with opioid or alcohol use."

Neuroreceptors and Health

I knew I found the ultimate health book when neuroreceptors in the brain were addressed in the first chapter. The author of *Boundless Energy*, Ben Greenfield, is known in the health industry for pioneering ways to optimize health through habits, nutrition, exercises as well technological innovations which is referred to as bio-hacking. He is a physical testament to how much he knows about human physiology and how to defy traditional aging. But when he named this first chapter "Coffee, Booze and Horror Flicks" with a deep dive into what these stimulants do to neurotransmitters (dopamine, acetylcholine, and GABA), I was sold on his expertise. With this single quote, I am going to open up a whole can of worms and attempt to explain what is happening in acute benzo withdrawals so that we may better understand what we need to do in the recovery stage to heal the damage. But before you rush out and buy his book, please understand that we are not ready to start or implement any of his techniques until we are in the later recovery stage or else risk a setback.

"When neurotransmitter activity in the gut or the brain is disrupted, the neurotransmitters in the other are also affected."

— Ben Greenfield

Our GABA receptors are everywhere, not only in the brain. When our bodies are imaged after being given something that attaches to the GABA receptors, the whole body literally "lights up like a Christmas tree." To find out that benzodiazepines work by attaching to the GABA A receptor is to fully realize how we got into the distressed states from prescribed long-term use. Those GABA neuroreceptors are the primary inhibitors to our entire central nervous system. We had anxiety or insomnia, and now, we have taken a prescription that caused damage to every part of our bodies from the nervous autonomic system (regulates breathing, heart rate and digestive) as well as our peripheral nerves (extending to our fingers and toes). This was done by the prescribed benzodiazepines that bound to the GABA receptors which opens a channel that allows chloride ion into the neurons causing sedation (according to a presentation from Colorado Consortium). This frequent opening of the neuron channels results in increased resistance to excitation (increased inhibition). Since the transmitter usually controls the opening and closing of the channel to the receptor but is over-ridden by artificial means of the medication, there is a compensatory reaction by the glutamate transmitter to make more the excitatory neurons. The homeostasis (balance of control) of the excitatory and inhibitory is disrupted and the body reacts by adjusting the operation of the GABA neuroreceptors.

Glutamate and the Unknown

Here is where things get murky as there is no evidence-based research on exactly what is now happening as tolerance sets in. We can give the anecdotal statement that we are no longer feeling the calming effects of benzodiazepine (either in intensity or duration) and that more medication is needed as our body starts to experience myriad physical and mental symptoms. But no imaging of the actual neuroreceptors exists with the current diagnostic technology. Brain CT scans only detect symmetry abnormalities, tumors or other lesions, infections, or bleeding. One theory is called neuroadaptation in which our bodies try to uncouple the GABA A receptor in a compensatory mechanism to get back to having only the amount of received GABA that our bodies transmitted which is called neuroadaptation.

Other theories suggest the GABA receptor downregulates its ability to absorb GABA (the calming neuron) and this is called down regulation of GABA receptors. As I stated, the diagnostic technology to confirm what is exactly going on is not obtainable, but the result is the same in both cases. We are no longer calm, and our bodies do not rest to regenerate and heal because of the increased active glutamate resulting from our bodies no longer being in homeostasis. And as Ben Greenfield's book states, "Other neurotransmitters are now being affected as well."

Glutamate is the excitatory neuron that allows us to react quickly to things. It promotes the excitatory impulse in our sympathetic nervous system that leads to the "fight or flight" state. While GABA's work is to relax our sympathetic nervous system, the glutamate does the opposite inducing the parasympathetic system to be on high alert. Is anyone feeling validated right now? Even though it is hard information to swallow, unlike the tiny pill we took, it was a bit of a relief to understand why fear and panic gripped me in acute despite having calm circumstances. We will address the social aspect or effect of benzo hell in later chapters but it would be good to point out here that it is theorized that people who have autism have high levels of glutamate in their bodies as well. Their need to self-soothe more than others who are not on the spectrum more sense to me too as well as their inability to deal with change as easily. After having been through benzo hell, I understand that airport scene from Rainman with Tom Cruise's character trying to get Dustin Hoffman's character to board the plane with much more empathy. I couldn't even look at pictures of mountains when I was in acute due to it bringing about such a state of fear that I was going to fall off. I now ski on mountains at 14,000 feet like I used to, so stick with me and read how these fears and phobias go away with healing. Also, nerve pain is shown to result from too much glutamate (hence the Gabapentin prescription that often follows tolerance), so this all started making sense to me as I hope it is for you.

How many people are prescribed benzodiazepines long term?

How many people are taking benzodiazepines in the US? According to the Colorado Consortium, prescriptions doubled from 2003 to 2015. I am going to suggest that they probably doubled again with the COVID pandemic. A simple Google search shows that 12.5 percent of the US population has or had a prescription for benzodiazepines (statistic from National Institute on Drug Abuse). That would be 30.5 million people. In total, it is estimated that there are more than 6 billion prescriptions written for benzodiazepines world-wide. Prescriptions mean ongoing usage.

There are real reasons for benzodiazepines to be used for short-term medical use in the hospital setting or in an emergency. Some examples are when a person becomes catatonic due to an emotional state such as grief, for preventing a seizure while rapidly or stopping alcohol for alcoholics, short-term sedation for a medically invasive procedure that a patient can't tolerate without such assistance and (please feel free to see the irony here) to reverse acute muscle rigidity or dystonia brought on by antipsychotic medication. Benzodiazepines are not a long-term solution for epilepsy as one may be told if they are in that situation or a family member is. Rather, this medication was prescribed when far more safer alternatives exist, but now, the patient is dependent on the benzodiazepines, and the doctor simply can't or won't deprescribe safely.

I will be completely honest here and say that if I had not had such the experience of being prescribed Ativan as needed but then started taking it more often during a highly stressful time then I would consider a prescription of this medication given to an individual who only uses it for occasional anxiety (like traveling by airplane) to be acceptable. However, I am saying that with huge trepidation as taking it for other life circumstances becomes the downfall that is not so easily avoidable when it is readily available in your home. And if the prescriber refuses to refill such an as needed prescription, that person is now having to source the benzo from the streets to avoid acute and protracted withdrawals. We could now be labeled as addicts from having a prescribed dependency that has happened because we supposedly abused a medication that was prescribed to take daily. This leads to doctor shopping to get new prescriptions rather than the help people need to get through benzo hell.

Benzodiazepines Cause Long-Term Disability in Many Cases

I believe that these prescriptions are not only contributing to decreased life expectancy but are causing much of the long-term disabilities that rob people of the quality of life in later years. I am also convinced that benzodiazepine prescriptions are causing marriages to fail, families to be cut off from each other, and even play a role in the increase of violent crimes. My family almost fell apart. My rage was uncontrollable during tolerance, and then I had no capacity to care for my children during acute. Only those who have experienced withdrawals can attest to the depth of Hell that we go to with this journey. When I finally was able to go back to see that psychiatrist in her office after about five months after my rapid detox and tried to explain how much I suffered and how much I learned, I was met with the response, "You are the only patient that I have ever had who has had such a negative experience." I knew that it was a lie as I had been in touch with other patients. Here is the deal: most doctors don't want to recognize that they have caused this damage and have no real medical understanding of how to properly taper and support people coming off benzodiazepines.

The outdated statistic that only 10 to 20% of people discontinuing long-term use of benzodiazepines have severe withdrawal symptom has been reversed in its entirety in the last few years. It is now estimated that only about 20 percent of people are spared any negative withdrawal symptoms after long-term use being defined as more than three months. The reality is that while there were huge gains in making this benzo hell more public in recent years, no one knows for sure what or how these drugs affect us long-term as Big Pharma has no reason to do such research. Little do they know, if they developed a pill to reverse all the damage to the GABA and other neurotransmitters affected by long-term use, they would have currently 30.5 million customers.

Some Doctors Are Heroes

There is one doctor who made a huge impact in exposing this shameful epidemic practice of prescribing benzodiazepines long term and her name was Prof. Heather Ashton (1929 to 2021). She opened a clinic in Britain in 1991 after seeing a pattern with patients experiencing harrowing symptoms when coming off benzodiazepines. Her work led to the highly valued and best resource that we have today: The Ashton Manual. And she made it her mission to make this resource free to anyone and everyone. The manual can be downloaded for free from Reference A under Resources on my website.

I will be referring to her manual often in the next chapters with more detail and insight on practical ways to apply her findings.

Very kind and compassionate doctors are picking up where she left off with what grant funds and university labs' budgets are available. Dr. Steven Wright is one of these doctors and served as the medical director for the Alliance of Benzodiazepines Best Practices from 2017 to 2021. I had the pleasure of speaking directly with Dr. Steven Wright early in my journey through benzo hell as he called me after I emailed him. He was a prescriber of benzodiazepines for decades before becoming "benzo-wise" and has done an amazing job to reform the prescribing practices by education, speaking on the topic in medical forums, and imploring others to take an active role in research of the injury that results from prescribed long-term use. This is a direct quote from him that is posted on the Benzo Information Coalition website www.BenzoInfo.com, "To all the benzodiazepine survivors who kept courage when we weren't listening and to all those who did not survive, I apologize. And here is a link I want you to share with others who may not believe you about being in benzo hell as it clearly shows that even he, as a prescribing practitioner, didn't know the extent of the damage being done by long-term use". Reference L under Resources on my website.

The Only Study into Why Some Suffer Protracted Withdrawals

Dr. Steven Wright emailed me a medical hypothesis written by Stephen LaCorte JD, who is a director at the Benzo Information Coalition. This document is linked under M Reference on my website under Resources. The title of it is *How chronic administration of benzodiazepines leads to unexplained chronic illness: A hypothesis*. It provides theory as to why people remain chronically ill for many years after long-term benzodiazepine use.

Flashback: I felt like I was ninety years old in acute and certainly moved like a geriatric patient riddled with disease. My body hunched over in fear, my weak legs wobbled, my balance was such that any disruption on the ground surface caused me to tumble, and the sheer pain in my joints and muscles made me act like that old person at only forty-seven years old. These symptoms can be explained as having the flu on steroids for those who can't relate or have never been in benzo hell. I am an athlete and back competing in sports. But had I gone to the doctor in that state (by then I knew not to and what was going on), I would surely have been diagnosed with a neurological disease and be on disability right now. But how did I pull out of this awful state while others remain in it for many more years and some even for life? That is the billion-dollar question, but reading his provisional study into what may be causing this not only makes sense in terms of what is technically happening but is essentially what my protocol is grounded in without even having the means to fully evaluate the efficacy of this proposed theory. "Mystery ailments including PWS may be at least in part be NO/ONOO (-) cycle illnesses." PWS stands for Protracted Withdrawal Syndrome which is we are referring to as part of benzo hell. Before I give you my interpretation of this study as well as highlight the conclusions of the meta-analysis research, I need to be clear that I am not even close to being educated enough to understand all the logistics of what is being discussed relative to that statement.

Recall that benzodiazepines are effectively opening a GABA channel allowing more chloride to come and increasing the potential energy between the transmitter and the receptor. That increase in potential energy leads to more inhibition and calming. When the benzodiazepine is taken away due to abrupt cessation or tapering off the medication, these neurotransmitters don't have enough GABA and we essentially freak out. But what our bodies eventually do by trying to reach homeostasis is they start generating our GABA again or more precisely the ability to absorb the GABA. It is a slow process as we suffer with the glutamate storm that we call benzo hell. But what the study proposes is that an electrical potential remains in these neurotransmitters like a valve stuck open. With all the symptoms and stress from this open channel without the ability to absorb GABA to regulate our sympathetic nervous system, chronic illness sets in many different forms. My protocol for healing from benzo withdrawals aims to close those channels so that a person can be healthy again.

Kindling Confirmed

The information in this article also confirms the phenomenon of kindling which is conclusively shown to extend the intensity and duration of benzo hell. I had never heard of this term "kindling" prior to this horrible experience other than when kindling was used to start a fire, or something was "rekindled" by external means. But it makes perfect sense now as "kindling" happens when (someone like me) uses benzodiazepines on and off (as needed), takes them for prolonged periods of time and the stops to only start again and/or starts a taper but then up doses due to not being able to handle the symptoms. Mice that were given benzodiazepines on a start and stop schedule with time between continuous dosing were much slower to heal and showed more intense symptoms of distress. This concludes that we are doing more damage when we kindle and is what I will try to avoid for others by writing this resource.

The article also suggests that elevated levels of peroxynitrite which causes downstream events like hypoxia and cell death are the by-products of this NO/OON perpetuated cycle. The excess amount of peroxynitrite could explain the extreme inflammation and sensitivity to everything that we feel in acute as our body fights the toxin. It also suggests that peroxynitrite can disrupt the mitochondria function in cells causing the endless fatigue. It proposes a risk factor to the cycle that may cause chronic illness could be a deficiency in tetrahydrobiopterin (BH4). BH4 is a naturally occurring nutrient that is required for the proper operation of other neurotransmitters such as for serotonin and dopamine which help with bodily functions such as sleep and mood. When I first was given this article my immediate "mad-dog" focus on what supplement could alleviate this BH4 deficiency but what I have learned over the last three years of research and experimentation is that there are natural ways to boost BH4 as well as to prevent the depletion of it due the noted cycle.

While there are still many unknowns as to why we suffer so hideously in benzo hell, there is one thing that I do know. We *need* more clinical research on how to heal from this iatrogenic injury. This is my call to action as there is much to be gained by finding solutions to helping people out of benzo hell and preventing more long-term disability. My focus is on the individual's ability to heal as my own investigation into technically was caused and what can heal this injury is ongoing. Referring back to Boundless Energy by Ben Greenfield with his quote pretty much sums up that no one should be put on a medication that changes selected neurotransmitters but especially due to the fact that one never knows how this medication works with other neurotransmitters responsible for cell communication.

Chapter 5
Preparation for Journey

There is no right or wrong way to get through benzo hell, but I have found that there is a more efficient way. It requires a mindset that uses radical acceptance, which takes a process to achieve. Radical acceptance is complete acknowledgement of reality even if it is not something that is easy to understand or believe. This rather new-age term and mindset was not easy for me to use initially as I am by nature a conservative person and by education a science-based believer. Prior to this injury, my main goals in life were obtaining materialistic things and states of physical pleasure with the perseverance of hard work. That changed as I had radically accepted my limitations due to this iatrogenic as part of the healing process in order to get positive results. Therefore I have concluded that radical acceptance is needed to start and successfully finish the journey through benzo hell. In this context, radical acceptance means we do have this iatrogenic (medically induced) injury as described in the previous chapter and that we have the power to heal ourselves. Let me be clear as we are not accepting the awful withdrawal state of being in benzo hell but rather that these symptoms are part of healing and that suffering is part of getting our health back. We are not being punished and do not deserve this. It is simply that there is no way around or under the healing process. We must go through it. That is why I called this book getting through benzo hell.

What does radical acceptance look like?

No matter where you are in your journey; a difficult decision to prioritize your health must be made. You can't pretend to feel okay with others and keep up your daily schedule with a good face and accept the healing symptoms at the same time. There will be a time for "faking until you make it" but this doesn't start until the worst of the experience is past and you are re-entering society (Chapter 10). After much reflection and listening to many other benzo warriors' journeys, I believe that the exact circumstances that lead us to use benzodiazepines need to be either methodically reversed or will be due to the illness of withdrawals. I am not even remotely suggesting an overhaul of your life is needed to survive but changes need to be made "moving the needle" in the right direction of prioritizing your health above anything else for this period and maybe forever. If you don't think that you were pushing yourself past a physiological limit like I was with my story, then we can agree to disagree and move forward with how to prepare for this journey but please note that efficiency of healing is my main goal.

It is completely up to you to decide how to prioritize your health. All I know is that we need this time and energy to heal and that this is much more available without the burdens of trying to maintain your old lifestyle. If you are the soul responsible caretaker of dependent people like children, then it is time to find some help. If you are managing a business with deadlines and/or people to manage, then you may need to back off from your responsibilities by delegating or closing shop temporarily. Whatever made you need this medication that caused the stress that led to the anxiety in the first place needs to stop. But here is the beauty of all this: you will be stronger mentally, tougher emotionally and physically healthier after getting through benzo hell so whatever you want to accomplish will be more possible and even better; you will enjoy whatever it is and it will be more meaningful to you.

Avoid Detox Centers

The absolute worst decision for anyone who is currently dependent on benzodiazepines is to go to a drug detox center. Many of the horror stories of people suffering protracted horrific withdrawals started this way. One of my very first clients survived a medical detox but then continued to have horrific symptoms for years after. My near fatal and despicably long recovery was caused by my foolish rapid detox but what saved me was being brought home where I was comfortable. The clinical environment of a hospital or medical facility with artificial lights and cleaning chemicals would be enough to cause us more damage during the process but that is not the only reason for this recommendation to stay home.

Our nervous system needs a familiar, safe environment to heal without as little outside stimulation as possible. This is not an opioid withdrawal where you are sick for a few days and get better within a few weeks. This is not an alcohol withdrawal where we need people and constraints from keeping us from taking the drug. We do not need intensive or regimented therapy during benzo hell as this process as it requires the opposite. There again could be a time for such psychological help but not during benzo withdrawals.

The process of either tapering or having an abrupt cessation of the medication can create the feeling of losing your mind but know that this is part of the recovery and not a developed mental illness. There is likely going more stress to our bodies and brain than we can feel that we can handle so our one and only objective to deal with that is to feel as safe as possible. Now if this means that you need to leave the place where you currently reside then in the most heroic but sometimes appearing weak with selfishness; you may have to find another place to live. It is not a decision to be made lightly and takes you being the hero to save yourself. I will tell you how I came to that exact decision myself.

I Moved Out

After getting mostly through the acute stage of benzo hell, I was minimally functional, but any required responsibilities, physical exertion, and mental stress would still produce massive waves. I was faced with the ultimate decision to leave my family. It was a difficult decision that did produce trauma for our children and almost ended in divorce. But I had no choice if I was going to implement the protocol to heal as efficiently as possible. Again, my aunt was supporting me, so at least I had a family member who understood and encouraged me prioritizing my health over literally everything else. But what instigated this decision was a post on BenzoBuddies.org by my friend Nate who asked the question: "If you could have enough money to do or buy anything that would help you heal from this injury then what would you do or buy." We had been discussing that even the rich and famous people were suffering as much as we were in benzo hell. All their money wasn't helping them to find a way around, over or under this iatrogenic industry (more on that later about Jordan Peterson).

Many of my insights that I share come from our community sharing their experiences and questions and this was a game changer for me. I knew I had to leave my house. It was a toxic environment that I had contributed to while in tolerance with my raging and that I desperately wanted to fix. But I had to get myself healthy first before I could contend with those family issues. I rented an apartment twelve miles away in a straight shot down Ocean Blvd (not difficult to get to is my point) for six months at the start of month four of my recovery. It is important to note two things.

1. Everyone's timeline in healing is different so do not take this as a recommendation for you
2. Had I done a proper taper and wasn't so badly injured that I was becoming chronically ill; I would not have had to do this.

This was part of my radical acceptance of prioritizing my health and thankfully our family is now back together again and working toward being peaceful and kind to each other.

Do Not Try to Do Damage Control until You Are Out of Acute Far along into Recovery stage

Much of what I advise on getting through benzo hell has to do with what not to do or what to avoid. This is one of the biggest ones to avoid doing. As we become more aware of how much of life, we were not living by coming off benzodiazepines and realizing what the sedative medication was doing to our relationships, we feel the need to analyze and make sense of what has happened in those months, years and/or decades of being medicated. That happens naturally. It can be devastating as the veil lifts, and we clearly see the wreckage of our lives as well as missed opportunities for happiness. Now is not the time to process this.

This book focuses on the critical time of the recovery stage after acute withdrawals as I explained. Recovering from this injury is about you and not fixing relationships with others. That work takes effort and energy that we simply do not have right now. This is not me being directive yet is me giving you that needed permission to wait and know that amending will come later. And quite frankly, without proper time and space for healing; you may end up making whatever relationship you feel compelled to address worse. I learned this the hard way with my mother who I have had issues with for much of my life. I hadn't been able to recognize and give her credit for being a fantastic Mom on practical matters but had been upset at her about her inability to be emotionally nurturing. I realized this when coming off benzodiazepines, but I totally botched that attempt when I tried too early in my recovery to make amends. It was a disaster and made things worse. Learn from me please.

Equally important to making the right decision to prioritize your health is to avoid making large life decisions during this time until you are recovered enough to do them with rational thinking. It will be tempting to do this as we see sources of our stress clearly and jump to eliminate or change them. How to delineate between decisions to prioritize your healing and other life decisions comes to whether these changes are reversible or not. There will more than likely be a way to deal with these stressors differently so don't be making irreversible changes to your life now. If you are considering a divorce, moving your family or becoming a Nun (kidding?); wait at least six months until after you feel healed to do such things. My decision to move out of my family home could have caused a permanent outcome but that was a risk I had to take to survive.

All decisions made to survive benzo hell are considered necessary and not optional. I share the following story in hopes of communicating how important it is to prepare for this journey through benzo hell. I would never share her real name, but she was a young mother who also was the primary caregiver for her ailing mother. It was truly the worst situation for healing as she felt she had no options or help as her husband worked as the breadwinner for the family and had little to no time to support her healing process. We were communicating online long before I decided to become a benzo recovery health coach, and I was still much impaired with my injury. She had done a three month taper off long term use of benzodiazepines but was still suffering in acute due to not having the time and energy to heal. She felt she had no options other than death. She told me that she was suicidal and all I could say at the time was to hang on. I felt her becoming more and more desperate with her writing until I didn't hear from her at all. It was her suicide (a permanent decision) that brought an end to her suffering but also ended her life and what could have been. Had she been better prepared for this horrific journey or she accepted that she needed care and support more than her mother and child then she might still be here. This is a temporary state of healing. It is not permanent.

Do not make permanent decisions.

What I now know and can offer advice on is how to prepare for this journey to avoid such tragedies. It is going to take courage to do this but hopefully you can see how important it is. If you are overburdened with responsibilities that are non-negotiable to let go then get help. Not the type of help that you must manage as that is not help in the long run. Remember that you will be healthier and more able to do things when you recover so think of this as giving yourself the time and space to heal without shame for having to ask. This may be much easier said than done as many of us have isolated ourselves by this time without even realizing it. I certainly had.

I had let my close relationships that would have been able to support my needs slip away in those three and half years of daily benzodiazepine use. However, I have an energetic husband who could (mostly) handle our family's needs while I was bed-ridden and after I moved out. He isn't perfect in terms of his limited capacity to have compassion but he more than made up for that in his ability to keep the house running while also running our business. I am grateful for that. Whether you have this resource readily available to you or not, it is up to you to find some support if you need it. Reach out for this support preferably before you start this journey getting through benzo hell. And if you feel like you have no one or can't pay for services then it is time to dig deep and find a way.

I would love to say that it is easy to find such support and give you a way to do that, but it is up to you and again, it depends on you prioritizing your health in order to do that. I support people finding such help in my practice by being a sounding board and offering feedback as some seek members of the church to help with childcare, find other parents to help with driving kids, and ask neighbors for meals to be cooked for them. I can tell you this with confidence though – you will never minimize the importance of community after this experience and I am working hard to re-establish mine by giving support to others as much as I can without negatively affecting my health.

Explaining What is Happening to Other People

How to explain to others what you are going through is another decision that I hope you prepare for. It is stressful enough being in pain so by planning ahead and warning family members; you may help them to understand how to best support you before the suffering becomes difficult to manage. I finally started telling people after about eight weeks from my jump that I had a chemical brain injury. Before that I was just MIA. Telling people about my dependence on benzodiazepines and the subsequent injury did scare some people off who I thought were my friends but were not. The fact that they would rather judge me for taking this medication over having compassion for my suffering was on them. Oh well. If there is anything that getting through benzo hell teaches you is that people who leave you when you are sick do not deserve your friendship.

It is going to be your call on how to explain what is going on while you recover. I am simply suggesting that you be honest that you have or will be healing from a brain injury. But try not make it your mission to make them understand everything about being dependent on benzodiazepines while you are suffering (which adds more stress). Educating your friends and family on benzo hell for a different reason, other than to support you, may also be part of this recovery but not now. Right now, it is about creating the safest, stress-free as possible for healing.

Full Health Checkup and Blood Panel

I will address whether to include your prescribing doctor in your decision to get off benzodiazepines in the next chapter on tapering. But, if possible, what I want you to do in preparation for this journey off benzodiazepines is get a full physical (including blood work) before you start this process of tapering off your benzodiazepine prescription. A big part of the success in getting through benzo hell is knowing that what you are feeling are just symptoms of your body re-regulating itself and not that you have something else wrong with you. Trips to the emergency room are frequent in benzo hell with people not knowing why their heart is racing (POTS) and/or they experience extreme panic attacks thinking that they are dying. This leads to unnecessary medical diagnostics that only create more stress.

It is quite common to be convinced they have now developed a new health issue or MS. We reviewed all this in Chapter 1, but I think that it is imperative now to get your health baseline before or soon after (not in acute) starting the withdrawal process so that you are not chasing symptoms and making yourself feel worse. Also, if your primary care physician is involved (if you choose to make them in your ongoing monitoring) in this check-up before the tapering begins, they can also provide checkups while you are in benzo hell. The check-ups could be used to assure you that you are not dying without them trying to find a source for the new symptoms which could lead you to a misdiagnosis of a neurological disorder that you don't have. Much of my coaching for people who are considering and/or doing medical interventions to deal with their symptoms in hopes of getting relief is to make them understand that there is no way around, under or over benzo hell and imploring them not to make themselves worse. It isn't a trivial matter as some have pre-existing conditions that were made worse by withdrawals. Having said that, if you didn't have the ailment before tolerance or withdrawals then it is my belief with 99 percent accuracy your awful symptom is from downregulated or decoupled GABA receptors.

Benzo Hell Awaits – Acceptance is Key

If you are already in acute benzo withdrawals, then please read this carefully. You will heal from these miserable symptoms and get through benzo hell regardless of whether you planned accordingly or not. I did. And if you are just at the stage of coming up with a plan to get off prescribed long-term benzodiazepines, you are most likely going to feel sick to some degree. The symptoms listed in Chapter 1 are coming even if you have not had them in tolerance. You will feel like you have the flu, and it will appear that your body is aging rapidly for a period of time. You may avoid the worst of it by doing this a much more controlled way with proper tapering but unless you are part of the estimated 20 percent with no symptoms at all, you will suffer. And then you will feel reborn. Accept that or the journey is going to be a lot harder for you. It was for me. I would not have survived without my aunt guiding me and encouraging me to actively retrain my brain without causing further damage. That is why I am doing what I am doing now by writing this book. Be prepared to suffer and be reborn.

DE Foster Benzo Free Podcast

If there is one resource that I would recommend as being invaluable for getting through benzo hell, it would be the free Benzo Free podcast by DE Foster. It is listed as Reference O on my website. He has over 100 episodes to date and each one offers support, insight, compassion, humor and education on what we are going through. He is a true benzo warrior as his recovery isn't complete after five years but has been through the worst of it to know that what people need most is validation. I shared my story in October of 2019 in my voice (Episode #43). Speaking of which, you will find his deep baritone voice soothing as I listen to the episodes at night to relax. D's podcast has provided enormous comfort for this community by sharing what he has learned about withdrawals and how to deal with anxiety in general. His information is timely and relevant as he regularly has experts on his podcast addressing specific symptoms and stages of benzo hell. What I appreciate most about Benzo Free Podcast is his honesty and relatability. I am not hiding anything about my experience through benzo hell in this book and he isn't either in his Podcast. The truth isn't that there is a quick solution or anecdote to the symptoms but a way of dealing benzo hell that makes us more resilient than we ever were before. That being said, the podcast contains triggering accounts of such suffering that it is probably safer to have been exposed to the reality of withdrawals before in it.

Chapter 6
Proper Tapering for You

This chapter provides insight and information for you to create for their tapering schedule based on their unique situation. The reduction of the benzodiazepine is called a tapering schedule. I review the gold standard of reducing the benzodiazepine while explaining how I have modified to make in more practical in application with my guidelines. Consideration to who is in benzo hell and the resources available personalizes the taper schedule. You will determine the best tapering schedule and method based on the on the advantages and pitfalls of different methods using dry cutting verse liquid titration. What I am ensuring with this information is that the taper will be medically safe while optimizing the recovery stage but what I cannot guarantee is that my suggestion will lessen the pain of getting through benzo hell. This is not something we can avoid unless we are blessed with either DNA that has provided the means readily to upregulate GABA receptors or you had not reached a point of being dependent on this medication.

There are four considerations to be considered when deciding the best method and rate of tapering off prescribed long term benzodiazepine use.

1. Current dose and availability of that dose
2. How long you have been on the daily use of the benzodiazepine
3. Urgency of Situation regarding Your Health/ Resources Readily Available for Support
4. Whether you will be working with a benzo-wise prescriber willing to work with you

My Hypothetically Correct Taper Plan

Using my answers to the above considerations I will explain how I would have tapered now given all that I know about benzo hell. It is a hypothetical plan that if

I had been able to implement could have saved me years of suffering. Recall that I did a foolish ten-day detox approved by my psychiatrist instead. But I do have to admit something that could have seriously impacted my ability to follow through on this taper plan. The pain and suffering from the interdose withdrawal from Ativan after I had used it continuously was seriously debilitating on its own. Therefore, if I had known or even thought that this proper taper plan off the Clonazepam was going to be even worse with such symptoms but still hadn't known about the protracted state that takes place due to abruptly stopping this medication; I probably would have done a much faster taper than what I am proposing now. My point is that we all have our individual limits and ability to deal with pain. I am admitting that I may not have been able to handle such a tapering plan to enforce that how you taper is your decision and what is considered technically proper could not be the best plan for you.

My situation was that I had been on 1.0 mg of Clonazepam (0.5 mg twice a day) for three and half years but had used 0.5 Ativan as needed for ten years prior (four to five times a month until my new Math teaching career began). The 1.0 mg

Clonazepam that I was prescribed was four times stronger than the 0.5 mg of Ativan that I had been using as needed. We will address varying strengths of each benzodiazepine later in this Chapter. But for those who are wondering why my doctor increased the dose by that much (even though I didn't even know these drugs were both benzodiazepines and I was not told of the up dosing scheme); I will be blunt and simply state that most doctors don't have a clue what they are doing or know that the varying strengths of 1 mg of each benzodiazepine can be as great as two times the amount. I would have never told my psychiatrist that I was starting a taper and therefore would have been happily given endless prescription refills by her.

It was urgent that I start due to my family situation, but I could have prepared outside help to support me with household duties to come off this medication. I would have known the Ashton method of reduction (will be explained) of shaving off 10 percent of the pill to 0. However, I was cognitively impaired by this time and in no way had the patience or capability of using a jewelry scale to obtain that level of accuracy. Therefore, the most repeatable and accurate measurement that I had available was ¼ of a 0.5 mg pill which is 0.125 (⅛) mg of Clonazepam. Given this personal information, this is how my taper plan should have gone.

Taper Plan for Jenny Karnacewicz (Starting Dose 1mg of Klonopin 0.5mg twice a day):

Reduce by ¼ of a pill (each dose) every fifteen days (Total Taper 115 days).

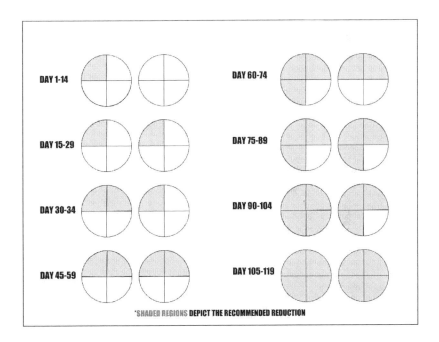

The circles are the pills that are physically quartered either manually or with the help of a pill cutter. The unshaded parts of the pill are the dosage while the shaded is the reduction. You can see that there will be remaining quarters to use on the next step down so that discarding them is based on how many you have and if you want to keep a reserve. Note that days 105-119 are showing no dosage taken but these days are still very critical to your taper and should not be considered being off the medication. Due to the half-life, the medication remains in the system, and I would have been very careful in those final days of the taper to protect my central nervous system.

I wish I could just insert a link to a spreadsheet tool that generated the optimal tapering schedule for you based on your current dosage of benzodiazepine and time on it. Being proficient in Excel and having generated such plans for other people, this would be quite easy. However, it is not legally advisable for me to do this as part of publishing this book. I am not a trained medical practitioner. And although I believe that my guidelines are safe and the best way to taper efficiently, there is a certain amount of responsibility that I cannot assume if I did provide such an excel link.

The Gold Standard of Tapering: Ashton Manual

What we do have available is the free Ashton Manual that I referenced in an earlier chapter. It offers sample plans as well as Prof. Ashton Manual recommendation of tapering long-term use of benzodiazepines at a rate of 10 percent reduction every ten to fourteen days. I totally agree that this would be an ideal way to taper if we have resources and time to do this properly but often, we don't. She did clinical studies with over thrBenzoBuddies.orge as well as follow-up contacts with hundreds more to determine this gold standard of reducing by 10 percent every ten to fourteen days. Here is an example calculation but you will find out that this ideal reduction method is not practical to implement for a number of reasons.

Reduction Example: Starting Dose 1 mg Klonopin; 1st reduction of 10 percent = 1mg*.10 = .1, New Dose is 1mg-.1 = 0.9 mg. If the person is taking 0.5 mg of Klonopin twice a day then that reduction would come from both doses such that the new doses would be 0.9 divided by 2 = 0.45 mg.

Her method of tapering keeps the original 10% of the original dose as the consistent reduction. Knowing what I do now about pharmacology and its affects on both the neurotransmitter and receptors after long-term use of psychotropic medication, the ideal reduction would be 10% of the last dose and not that consistent 0.1 from the example provided. She has published other example withdrawals plans from various types of benzodiazepines and dosage in the Ashton Manual that also include switching to a longer acting benzodiazpine (Valium or Diazepam). Reference A under Chapter two of Slow Withdrawal Schedules.

Why I Don't Recommend Using the Exact Ashton Method for Practical Reasons

Here are the reasons why I am not recommending such a taper given what I have learned over the last four (4) years by working with others and being active in this community. In order to be able to get this reduction accurately from a tablet, one must use a jeweler scale which I purchased after my ordeal to test the feasibility of using it for following the Ashton method. Using such a scale involves the delicate procedure of zeroing it properly (using known weights) as well being able to shave off just enough material from the pill to get the correct reduction dose. It is not an easy task but can be done if you have the patience and ability to learn. Many of us are impaired both cognitively and with hand dexterity by the time we are attempting to get off this medication and therefore using this method is difficult to begin with. And of course, the scale has to be purchased as an added expense (which will not be covered by insurance) and it is equipment that can break easily due to a misshapen accident. I didn't break mine while testing it, but I could see how this could happen quite easily if I had been in withdrawals at the time. Then there is a technical process to "zero" the scale. But then there is a whole other hurdle in that the pills/tablets do not weigh the same as the dosage (1mg Klonopin doesn't weigh 1 mg) so that the starting dose weight needs to be used and that is what is reduced. **The reduction example given would not work as it is only a dosage reduction and not the required weight reduction that the user needs in order to taper properly.** Then some of the pill/tablets don't weigh the same and more calculations per dose need to be done. If this type of complicated dry cutting works for you then great but it didn't with most of my clients and lead to a lot of confusion on BenzoBuddies.org.

Liquid Titration

What was just discussed is called dry-cutting as it uses the original form of table that the benzodiazepine was prescribed in form. Another type of reduction uses liquid titration, and this can be even worse in terms of accuracy and complications although there are many who have successfully completed such a liquid titration taper. I am reviewing it to explain why it is not what I recommend and to clarify how it is done. The table is dissolved in a liquid and the reduction is made by "pulling" an amount of that liquid from the solution using a syringe. The first problem is that benzodiazepines are not liquid soluble in water. They do not dissolve in a constant manner and little particles of concentrated medication are left either at the bottom or the edges of the container. Some crush up the pill into a dust and then dissolve it using a spoon but this produces the same result in that you may have a better consistency in the solution for a second but as soon as the swirling is done – the particles settle and cling to the side of the container. An example of this would be dissolving 1mg of Klonopin in 10 mL of water and removing 1 ml to use the remaining 9 mL as the reduction dosage. But if benzodiazepines are not water soluble but do dissolve in alcohol then why not just use Vodka for this solution? I wish I was kidding when I say people ask and do this unbelievable foolish liquid tapering. We will get into how alcohol is the most important thing to avoid in the next chapter but let's leave it right now as I am going to assume that anyone smart enough to pick up the book will know not to mix a benzodiazepine in alcohol of any form.

Equivalency Benzodiazepine Table and Tapering Schedules

Equivalency Table for Common Benzodiazepines and Schedules for Tapering			
Schedule	I	II	III
Ativan (Lorazepam)	2 mg	4 mg	6 mg
Xanax (Alprazelam)	1 mg	2 mg	3 mg
Klonopin (Clonazepam)	1 mg	2 mg	3 mg
Valium (Diazepam)	20 mg	40 mg	60 mg

My Tapering Guidelines

This chapter is called Tapering for You because what I am going to recommend is that you decide the best tapering plan for you given what I have explained. I offer suggestions based on what is feasible due to the urgency of your health, what type of medication you are able to obtain (dry or liquid), life circumstances at the present and future time (availability of outside help) and/or your desire to be done with benzo hell as well as how you are handling the symptoms from these reductions. In that order. My guidelines for the length of tapering schedules are the following:

Schedule I: Up to the Equivalent of 20 mg of Valium per Day

If you have been on the benzodiazepine for a month then taper over one week.

If you have been on the benzodiazepine for more than one month, then taper one week per month.

If you have been on benzodiazepines for years, then taper one month per year.

If you have been on benzodiazepines for decades then taper one year per decade.

Schedule II: Up to the equivalent of 40 mg of Valium per day; Double the length of taper from the guidelines Ex: 2 mg of Klonopin; two years; Taper for four Months

Schedule III: Up to the equivalent of 60 mg of Valium per day; Triple the length of the taper from the guidelines Ex: 3 mg of Klonopin, two Years; Taper for six Months

These guidelines use the original dose that you are currently on with the reduction being the lowest, repeatable amount that can be obtained using a pill divider. This is so that no doctor or technology needs to be involved. The way to apply these guidelines is to use the lowest reduction available along with the suggested tapering time frame to create a taper plan that keeps the reduction rate as consistent as possible. I am not saying to avoid telling your doctor of your tapering plans but remember that as soon as doctors hear of plans to taper you may be subjected to being cut-off from your medication much quicker than you would like to be. (Recall that once my husband notified my psychiatrist that I was detoxing, she immediately cut off my prescription. ?!)

I am using days, weeks, and months as an accessible timeframe to taper safely but without dragging the process out any more than necessary. If anyone's absolute goal is to never feel a symptom and stay as far away from acute as possible then stretching the taper out could be helpful or (in many of my experiences supporting others) it could just prolong your baseline suffering. Recall that your baseline is the state where you are consistently feeling and not in a window or a wave as defined in Chapter 3. These suggestions could slowly change (not abruptly) as the person tapering either becomes much better without any adverse reactions or suddenly too ill to cope due to the aggressiveness of the taper.

If You Have a Benzo-Wise Doctor and Can Get Liquid Benzodiazepines

If you are lucky enough to have found a benzo-wise doctor who will work with you by prescribing a benzodiazepine in liquid form, then please take full advantage of this coveted and rare opportunity. Using a benzo liquid titration (this is not dissolving pills in water) is the best way to both accurately reduce and control the rate of tapering. However, it is still important that this doctor is open to letting you "hold" if you are going to use a symptom based taper or else you could run out of medication. I say that as a warning but most likely if a doctor is educated enough to understand the need to prescribe liquid benzodiazepines, then they probably know enough about the process to prescribe more of it than the minimum needed to complete taper. I can only hope that more and more people have this option as it provides the person tapering with much more resolution to make the smaller 10 percent cuts as recommended by the Ashton Manual.

My Thoughts on a Strictly Symptom-based Taper

We have Benzo warriors in this community who promote a symptom-based taper which means only reducing by an amount your body can tolerate avoiding as much as the horrible withdrawal symptoms as well as holding the dose (taking the same dose without reducing) for a longer period of time to stabilize before making a reduction. Dr. Christy Huff M.D. has been a fantastic advocate for benzo awareness and has written valuable articles educating both doctor and patients as well as having a Blog about her journey through benzo hell. Her Blog and story can be found on my Website under Reference P.

Dr. Huff used a symptom-based taper to get off 1.5 mg of Xanax that she had taken for approximately four months, and it ended up taking almost four years to taper off using Valium. As I touched on in Chapter 4, there are reasons to hold a taper that included necessary lifesaving medical procedures and she also had to do exactly that when she was diagnosed with breast cancer in year two. She continued her symptom-based taper even after having to address the cancer with a medical intervention. Why I am bringing her name up in this context is to illustrate why I am reluctant to subscribe to a symptom-based taper. Everyone does this their own way and I applaud anyone who is brave enough to share their journeys as we are a community that can learn from others to avoid making the same mistakes. While I am not aware of her ever acknowledging that this extremely long taper (after such short continuous use) created more suffering for her, she does document her deteriorating physical and mental health that continued even after the taper was complete.

I do know that she is now well on her way to regaining her health (as I follow her on Instagram) and am so happy and excited to see her health finally returning. But I used her public story to share my concern that she would have been able to preserve her health by getting off benzodiazepines much better using the structured plan using my suggested guidelines. While I fully recognize that my ten-day rapid detox was the most entirely stupid and risky way to get off almost fourteen years of using benzodiazepines and was most certainly was never the way to correctly taper. But my story (which is all documented in videos) compared her story with the amount of time suffering in benzo hell after deciding to get off these medications isn't even close. I may have felt like I lost my health entirely, but I remained healthy enough to start healing at about six months post jump. This is not a competition or a race to see who can get off benzodiazepines the quickest, but it is a learning experience to apply to your taper.

Where Am I in My Recovery

I am mostly recovered and living a life that is more meaningful than I ever had while taking this drug. I am healthy, functional and enjoy every day. I feel 90 percent recovered 90 percent of the time. The other 10 percent of the time I could feel anywhere from 50 to 75 percent recovered as waves continue to wash through (more on that later). I should have tapered over three-and-a-half months and if I had done that then I may not have had to spend three months in bed followed by intermittent days and weeks over the next three years in benzo hell. However, I would not be here if I had to sustain the level of pain and felt illness if I had to taper over much more than that three-and-a-half month time period. I am pretty sure I would have delayed each cut hoping to feel better and run out of hope. Everyone has their limit and I know mine. You need to know yours.

The exhaustion and bone aches that I was experiencing may have been less in a longer taper but for me that lessened pain would not have been worth suffering even longer. Also, it is a scary but true fact that there are a few people who taper for years and are still left chronically ill. I think that the body can only handle so much so it is better to front load the pain and suffering of a structured taper so that you have as much of your health for the journey through benzo hell. Some people don't make it out of acute due to the combination of the prolonged stress on their bodies combined with their age and pre-existing conditions. All I can say is that the better health that you have going into the tapering and keeping your health as much as you can is much more efficient than a slower symptom-based taper that may compromise your health further. You need to decide for yourself using the suggested guidelines.

When to Start Your Taper

When to start the taper is a whole other issue that needs to be addressed as well. Per my last Chapter, much preparation is needed if this journey off benzodiazepines is to be successful. Preparation of having the correct mindset with radical acceptance, confirming your physical health is adequate to sustain the stress of withdrawals and making sure your physical environment has the least amount of stress possible by getting the help and offloading responsibilities. I am just reminding you of this as most of us would like to get off these drugs as soon as possible after being told or discovering ourselves how much we have been damaged by them. So please start a taper that you can finish by waiting a few weeks or a couple months to start the process. D.E. Foster speaks on his podcast of his and his doctor's decision to delay the start of his taper as a much-needed way to make sure he was ready for this journey, and I commend this way of thinking. I will also go over diet changes to think about prior to starting this taper to best prepare your body and brain for this in the next Chapter.

However, if the benzodiazepine has turned paradoxical on you then the decision to start tapering may not be up to you. Recall that paradoxical reactions are when your symptoms of suffering increase after each dose and subside before the next dose only to come back full force again with the next dose. This is the opposite of tolerance and needs to be understood as such. Your baseline in tolerance may be constant suffering but the symptoms don't get immediately worse with every dose. Again, as already discussed, your health needs to be as good as possible when starting this process so that means preserving what energy, vitality and positive mindset is of utmost importance. Please don't delay starting this process if this is you unless it is for a life-or-death matter.

Unfortunate Medical and Life Circumstances

Some unfortunate people do develop real and dangerous medical conditions during the tapering or withdrawal process that (seemingly) have nothing to do with the withdrawal process. The first time I was driving in benzo hell, I was met in the cul-de-sac by my father and my nieces in his car. They were coming to say goodbye to my daughter as she was leaving the next day for a trip to Spain. I didn't explain why I was driving but kept the interaction brief as I was shaking inside and out and out yet no one in the other car was able to notice. I was on my way to a scheduled doctor appointment to see a dermatologist about a bright red but painless skin condition on my right shin. I had sent a picture to the doctor asking whether I should come in or not explaining that I was gravely ill, and it would take a lot out of me to even make the trip. Of course, the people in the office had no clue what benzo withdrawals were but I was told that this skin condition (which was growing every day) was in fact the start of a skin cancer and I needed to be seen.

A quick Google search by my daughter showed that it was most likely a type of melanoma. I scheduled the appointment for the next day, but my husband was not available to take me. I hadn't been in touch with my parents for weeks now and my daughter could not drive yet. So, I tried my hardest but failed to be able to go as the story ends with me turning around and parking my car for the next month. I am sharing this story now to both illustrate how things like this do happen that if necessary medical intervention is needed then it is up to you to weigh the risk versus benefit before proceeding. I was lucky in my case. It was almost like divine intervention again that I had had a prescription in my bathroom drawer for another precancerous lesion from a couple of years ago. I used that topical creme three times a day for the next week and the lesion went away.

Flip side is that I had two clients with similar cancer-like lesions on their skin develop during tapering and/or withdrawals who chose to undergo surgery and ended up causing serious setbacks to their recovery from benzo hell. There could be decisions that you have to make in your journey like this, but the only sound advice I can give you is to hold on the taper process (keep the dose the same without reducing) if you have to have such a medical intervention. I was already in acute, so my decision was to either push myself and go see the doctor when I had someone to bring me or to use my resources to address the medical condition and I chose wisely for me.

Hiring a Benzo Recovery Health Coach

If you are still unsure of the best tapering method for you or need additional support, then please consider hiring a benzo coach. While there are ways to connect with other benzo warriors (Facebook Groups) and possibly find someone to help you without paying for their services, the availability and accountability of such an informal arrangement may not be enough support for you. I know that before I became a certified coach that I had many people contacting me for such support, but I was not able to keep up with the demand nor were most of them following through on my suggestions. Making it a professional arrangement has provided much benefit for the person needing the support and made me commit my time in a much professional manner.

I would like to share that much to my surprise and delight, I was contacted by a doctor who may be looking for benzo recovery coaches for her new practice that deals specifically with deprescribing from long-term use. We had a great conversation about the mind-body connection and her experience in treating addiction (which we clarified right away was not the same as benzo dependency). I told her that my next few months were entirely committed to completing this book and she said to get back in touch with her when it was a finished project.

I wrote this book in part to process and give closure to my own benzo hell experience. But my main goal in writing this book was to provide a protocol that includes tapering suggestions to help others to get through benzo hell. Whether this book is used in conjunction with my coaching or as a stand-alone resource, it has served its purpose as I move forward with reclaiming or finding new roles in life. I also give real-time updates on my recovery on my Instagram account benzorecovery.JennyK. My website is www. copperhealthcoach.com and will be offering on-line scheduling of appointments as well as a free gift if you read this book and answer the questions.

Final Comments on a Long Chapter

I don't want you to overthink your options on tapering your Benzodiazepines but just go with the one that feels the most doable without making a hasty or risky decision. If you already in tolerance or interdose withdrawals and therefore are in a constant state of stress then nothing is easy during this time so make this decision with a little internal debate as possible. I am currently working with a client who has postponed their taper for well over a year due to ruminating on what could happen, and it is obvious that her health is steadily declining. Your tapering plan should be created by you given all the information that I have provided but the follow through to succeed in the taper is also going to be entirely dependent on you. I don't think anyone would have imagined that we would be left to our resources to get off a medication prescribed by our doctors, but it is the reality. The reward from successfully tapering will be freedom from a pill causing you misery. And what you learn about yourself during the tapering will be equally amazing as the new person that is almost reborn after getting through benzo hell

Chapter 7
Nutrition (Fuel to Heal)

I am not a certified nutritionist, and I am not going to recommend a specific diet for you. I am just going to share what I found to be helpful for my healing as well as what I learned from other benzo warriors. While most of my recommendations seem to be in line with simple, practical healthy eating; I have found a few caveats of information about what to eat and when to eat that have seemed to help others in my coaching practice. The biggest gains in my recovery did not come from supplementation or strict limiting of certain foods but in the minimal and sustainable changes to my eating habits. Hence, I hope you can find ways to "move the needle" in your nutrition by reading what I share with you.

Acute: Don't Let Concern for Food Choice Become a Second Dart

If you are in acute and struggling to put any food at all into your mouth, then please know that your only job is to get down whatever you can when you can. Don't let the recommendations of eating clean be a "second dart" in this awful and already concerning state. The second dart is the reaction to the first dart. When I was having cortisol rushes in the morning and my mouth went completely dry, but I knew that protein would help my blood sugar, I made the mistake of trying to force food into my stomach. It rarely made it past my throat. What I should have done and done now when something prevents me from feeling hungry is accept that this is a transient state that will pass. Many people lose drastic amounts of weight in benzo hell but are able to (quite easily in fact) gain it back once they are out of acute. You may have this experience too. There are testimonies on BenzoBuddies.org of people who have fully recovered who could only eat processed foods like hot dogs and peppermint patties due to their developed food aversions. please be okay with your limited capacity to eat if that is happening if you stay hydrated. To stay hydrated, I learned that adding a carrier fluid to the water helps the hydration process, so I recommend a bit of cranberry or lemon juice to your water. It is after the state of acute that I will encourage you to start "moving the needle" toward whole foods and not before then. And just to be clear, I am not talking about sourcing purely organic ingredients and preparing gourmet meals. That would be near impossible given how you feel and what you can do in benzo hell.

Smoothie for Acute

My friend Jordan recommended this go-to smoothie for acute when eating was difficult for me and now I have dozens other clients drinking this as well. This smoothie is made with ¾ fresh or thawed frozen spinach, 1 cup almond milk, 1 cup coconut water (or plain water), 1 banana and ¼ cup yogurt (dairy free if desired). You can add any whole foods that you like such as frozen berries for both taste and their antioxidants. Blend these ingredients with some ice for a flavorful drink that you can sip on for clean calories. I had issues with using the blender in acute as the vibration of the motor spinning was literally too much for my central nervous system and often asked my family members to help me make these smoothies.

Transitioning to a Mostly Whole Food Diet in the Recovery Stage

I have concluded that good quality nutrition based on a whole foods diet rich in protein (as unprocessed as possible but not necessarily lean) and antioxidants will in fact expedite healing based not only on my experience but that of my clients. With small efforts made to eat whole foods and unprocessed meats, benzo warriors have reported feeling better both mentally and physically. But it is important to note that if your body is used to processed food and sugar then taking it away could abruptly cause even intensify withdrawal symptoms.

As I was attending a conference for the Health Coach Institute during my training, I noticed a fellow colleague in obvious pain and a distinct gait disruption that I had in acute. I asked three questions and immediately determined that she had been taking Ativan while caring for her dying husband (over a year) but had stopped a couple of months prior as she thought it was fine to do. She explained (without knowing what I did yet) that her husband had passed, and she was now on a mission to eat and be healthy and become a health coach. I asked what her diet was like while she was caring for her husband compared to now and she quickly admitted that she had cut out all sugar and processed foods about a month ago. I asked when the intense pain had started and she seemed to find a correlation right away with the diet change. I then explained who I was and what I did and we came up with a plan to add back some of her regular food in without being rigid about its nutritional value. Would you believe that I noticed her improve that week before my eyes? She wasn't healed from all of her pain but there were definite improvements so please be advised that if your diet is mainly processed food with sugar that you will have to take the transition to mostly whole foods slow in order for the body to re-regulate and digest properly.

Whole foods do not mean eliminating or limiting meat. The body needs protein to heal, and meat provides more protein (ounce per ounce) than plants. Plant food is important too as I will address when discussing micronutrients. A balanced diet that includes both plant and meat that are in the purest original form is what I am suggesting. The balance in this diet does not need to be equal between meat and plants but should include both. I highly recommend the pagan diet that Dr. Hyman promotes which is much in line with that I have found to be helpful. His diet is a hybrid between Paleo and Vegan and it is based on 75 percent nutrient dense plants and the remaining 25 percent of the protein from animals. I have known benzo warriors who claim that the keto diet has helped them tremendously, but I have also heard the opposite to be true for some. What I learned in my health coaching certification is that no diet is optimal for everyone and that your body is the best chemistry lab that provides you with the best feedback on what foods are helping and what are hurting you. Pay attention please.

Me: A Fast-Food Junkie

I was a fast-food junkie during tolerance of prescribed long-term use of benzodiazepines. How that happened was a result of not caring about my health due to the sedative properties of the medication and then my appetite or taste buds for whole foods became non-existent as processed foods and sweets became my preference. I would eat to not only satisfy my hunger but to also create a positive feeling that I so desperately lacked in my life. Just to show how much of a fast-food junkie I was and how messed up my thinking was in this acute stage, I will share an embarrassing story.

I had been relying on my husband and daughter for my food when in acute and they are healthy eaters by nature so that is what they were giving me to eat. But I wanted my comfort food and even demanded it. I called my aunt to tell her that they were starving me because no one would get McDonald's for me. Yup. I did that. But recall the only good thing that was noted was the awful ten-day detox except for my strange ability to taste good, natural food and desire for more of it. This was a blessing in that this would help me continue to make good food choices even when I could get food on my own. This new appreciation for quality of food also propelled me to eat kale out of my daughter's garden as I previously shared. All of this was before learning the benefits of the whole food diet which I will share with you.

Deficiencies in Nutrients After Prescribed Long-term Use of Benzodiazepines

It is proven that we become deficient in certain nutrients due to prescribed long-term use of benzodiazepines and the stressful experience of going through benzo hell. It could be a result of our bodies not being able to absorb them properly as well as how quickly they are used by the body to combat the oxidative stress (refer to Chapter 4 on Technically what is going on). It also could be that we ate like crap for years to combat the symptoms of being in tolerance like just I shared. Either way a mere google of what nutrients are depleted by benzos show that these nutrients include but are not limited to biotin, folate, calcium, melatonin, Vitamins D and K. Please do not run out and buy these supplements right away. Extreme care must be taken when supplementing that I will address soon. But for now, my goal is to encourage you to find what foods contain these nutrients as this is you helping yourself to heal.

As I said, your body is the best chemistry lab for you so use it to determine which foods with the needed nutrients appeal to you as well as what your body can digest. We can become highly sensitive to certain foods in benzo hell, and it is my hard learned lesson to only share what has helped me and not recommend specific food. For example, I found a great benefit to eating walnuts which are high in those needed nutrients but one of my clients (who had never eaten walnuts before) had a disastrous reaction to them which heightened his anxiety for many hours. Take it slow when trying new foods and don't eat them if they don't make you feel any better or worse.

Processed Food are Full of Neurotoxins

Having said that, I can safely say to try to avoid processed foods once you are out of acute and can fathom eating anything else (for those who relied on processed food to survive acute), The problem with processed food is not as much that the food is lacking in nutrients but that it is made to be preserved for a longer shelf life with chemicals. These artificial preservatives along with colors/dyes and sweeteners are in fact neurotoxins but are FDA approved for use due to the low concentrations in the products. I am not saying that there could be toxins in whole foods (like mercury in fresh tuna) but rather suggesting that the big picture is to move away from foods processed with added chemicals. It is not proven but plausible that our bodies are getting more of these toxins in the processed food than one normally does due to a compromised brain-blood barrier as well as a leaky gut. The blood-brain barrier is meant to protect the brain from such neurotoxins by being highly selective on what permeates through into the nervous system. But after having used prescribed long-term benzodiazepines which work by readily passing through the brain-blood barrier undetected, signs of neurotoxicity develop in benzo hell. The same for the gut in that the intestinal lining is meant to prevent certain toxins from entering the tissue and being circulated into the bloodstream. Since both these phenomena are speculation at this time, it would be safe to avoid processed foods when possible.

Benzo Belly

Another hideous symptom of benzo hell is benzo belly. It is not as funny as it sounds as our stomachs bloat as if we are close to being nine months pregnant (or how my friend Steven says – he sometimes looks like he is pregnant with twin ponies). Not that we can entirely avoid this, but we can help ourselves to heal from it by providing soluble fiber in the form of raw vegetables. Benzo belly is result of a disrupted microbiome when there are not sufficient acids or too much acid to properly digest food and it turns into gas causing extreme bloating. My theory on this is that excess yeast (Candida) is part of the culprit. During the worst of having benzo belly, I noticed that my tongue had a strange film on it. Some research turned up that it was thrush which is from excess yeast. I am not recommending this, but adding a couple drops of raw apple cider vinegar seems to help me with benzo belly. This symptom is not entirely gone for me yet and sometimes I get discouraged by it only to remember that I had made poor eating choices. I still eat some packaged goods from time to time but try to avoid them when possible.

Blood Disorder from Benzo Withdrawals

This next story may scare some people, but I am telling you to learn from it as we do not know the extent of the (reversible) damage that withdrawals from benzodiazepines can do to our biological functions. As I have stated, my most intense and long-lasting symptom was a deep bone ache. I had many blood panels over the years, so when a doctor (after acute in the recovery stage) suggested that I get my iron checked based on my symptoms of heaviness and aches; I was surprised that my ferrite and iron levels were so high that they ordered genetic testing. It came back that I had hemochromatosis, and it was advised that I start a blood-letting routine and change my diet. I saw my blood in the vials when I went in, and it even looked viscous and dark. I decided to do nothing as I weighed the risk and benefit of being subjected to the lab and needles which were difficult for me to handle. I got tested eight months later, and everything was normal. I got tested again recently, and there is no concern at all for my iron levels. That is my proof that we experience grave damage to our ability to digest food that can produce or allow toxic levels to increase in the blood. Many of my brain symptoms also abated about the same time as my physical ones and is when I went to get retested so I am convinced they are related.

Deep Dive into Micronutrients

I had always considered food in terms of the macros of fats, carbs and protein. Not anymore. There is a wealth of nutrition in things like basil, parsley, turmeric, chia seeds, honey, coco powder, and tons of other things that are eaten with macros that I had never considered to be important to health. Again, Dr. Hyman's podcast provided a wealth of information on this topic as he explains that food can be medicine with the use of "Farmacy instead of Pharmacy" in the name of his podcast. I am not going to do a deep dive into micronutrients here but want to encourage you to learn about them so you can enjoy finding them on your own. It has become kind of like a treasure hunt for me to find these sources of healing the body.

There is a micro-nutrient in broccoli, broccoli sprouts and other green leafy vegetables such as spinach and kale that may be especially important in benzo hell. Glutathione (GSH) is a neuroprotective that both protects cells from oxidant and helps cells excrete toxins. Ben Greenfield in *Boundless Energy* explains that in order for this GSH to work that there needs to be adequate protein which he refers being "0.5 to 0.8 g per pound of body weight, which equates to about 85 g to 136 g per day for a health 170 pound person" (p.79). I recommended a smoothie that has spinach in it for acute when eating is difficult, but that was based on how it made me, and other clients feel. I did not learn about this micronutrient until recently when listening to an Andrew Heuberman podcast. He provides excellent information on evidence-based research done on health and living as healthy as possible on his podcast but again, much of what works for normal people may not work for people who are in benzo hell or worse could make them worse. However, the recommendation of increasing this micronutrient has proved beneficial to many of my clients with almost immediate results. But having said that, digestion is already compromised so not overdoing it with too much leafy green is important too.

The Importance of Omega Fatty Acids

I certainly learned a ton about the importance of omega fatty acids and the ratios of Omega 6 to Omega 3 (1:1 to 4:1 where the American diet has been found to have this ratio as high as 15:1) in my health coaching certification, but it was when I started researching supplementation for brain injuries that I paid attention to this. With our brains being essentially 60 percent fat and the fact that our body doesn't make these essential fats found to be essential to blood flow, neurotransmitter communication, membrane structure, and growth in brain tissue to the brain, it makes sense that omega fatty acids are crucial for healing. The brain injury or even slight damage caused by artificially manipulating neuro-receptors with medication isn't detectable by imaging as I have discussed but the symptoms of brain fog, headache and bizarre sensations in our brain are proof enough that something is going on. I equate this brain damage to having a burn on the skin. Yes, the skin will heal over time, but putting an ointment that encourages the wound to heal while also protecting it is how I now view omega fatty Acids for this protocol on efficiently healing.

Omega 3s protect the brain from neurological conditions which are present in benzo hell. Foods that contain Omega 3 acids include oily fishes, like salmon, mackerel, and sardines, and nuts and seeds, like walnuts, chia seeds, and flaxseeds. I believe there is a great benefit to adding a high-quality fish oil supplement to my diet but was not able to do add or even try this supplement until month four after my jump due to extreme sensitivities and fear of causing more discomfort. Omega 6s help reduce inflammatory conditions which is also a large part of benzo hell. Food that contains Omega 6s include avocados, eggs, sunflower seeds, and cashew nuts. Omega 9s help with insulin sensitivity (glucose control) and also aid in decreasing inflammation. Food that contains Omega 9s include olive oil, almonds, hazelnuts, and pistachios. My clients who have "moved the needle" by incorporating more fats from these food sources have shown to be more efficient in their healing than those who have yet to be curious enough to make these small changes in their diet.

I stumbled across the use of the spice turmeric when I was in the recovery stage as I was just beginning to be able to cook for myself. My go-to meal was easy to prepare and used turmeric for both taste and its anti-inflammatory properties. It consisted of cooked, cold rice (that I would make in large quantities) reheated with fried eggs and sauteed onion in olive oil with turmeric and salt added for taste. Yes, this is called fried rice, but I had no intention or capability of following a recipe and knew that eating this would make me feel better without taking too much time standing. That is how I coach others to find out what types of meals that they can prepare will help them. I also noticed that white fish, like haddock and cod, were good at calming me down instead of revving my nervous system up as some other foods did. I have since learned that other benzo warriors have found that white fish lowers their cortisol rushes as well. My point is to be curious with the whole foods framework and repeat eating what you find gives you strength and energy while avoiding foods that you determine cause you more harm. Never liked brussel sprouts? Try them. Try them as Dr. Seuss would say, and you may find that you like them, Sam I am.

My Set Back at 18 Months Due in Part from Eating Poorly

I had a significant setback in my recovery during Christmas 2020 when I was at eighteen months after my ten-day detox due to poor eating choices. I had been feeling quite well for five months after a major wave at twelve months when I came home from Colorado to a huge Harry and David Holiday basket. The trip home was stressful, and there was much to do to get ready for hosting Christmas, which gave me the ridiculous excuse to dive into the packaged goodies. I was not strictly limiting myself to just whole foods at this point, but I was still being careful as it proved I should have been. From the cured meats with preservatives to the processed baked goods in the packages and all the sugar and artificial colors that went with it, I ate it all. My family left the day of Christmas to return to Colorado, and even though I had planned on staying home to take care of our home business and the dog, I would not have made the trip. I was bed bound again. I must note that there were stressful events during those few days before they left, andI had to race to their bus stop to the airport with luggage that was forgotten at home, but I felt the wave coming, and it slammed me for the next two weeks. Lesson learned, and I have not ever allowed such stress and bad eating to happen again.

Glutamate and Histamine in Foods

You may find extreme sensitivities to unexpected food choices as I did. I had not yet learned about glutamate or histamine issues from certain foods and even though I am aware of such issues now; I do not pretend or want to be an expert in these things. Your body is your responsibility. We figure out what is not helping and learn from it. That is my motto and also adheres to much of what I learned by attending my coaching certification classes at the Health Institute. But for me; I was hit with more bone aches and flu-like symptoms caused by bone broth and high gluten foods like bagels. When I was alerted that bone broth has glutamate and that was a real cause of my discomfort, I then started to be more aware of other foods high in glutamate like walnuts. I can eat anything now without hardship but being aware of this helped me avoid more distress. The gluten thing was strange though. I had always suffered stomach cramps when eating processed white bread even before benzo hell so I knew there was an issue already. But what I started reacting to was anything with gluten would cause my heart rate to increase and some lead to palpitations. This was not the symptom called POTS, which I will discuss in Chapter 8. I had real physiological reactions to gluten that seem to be connected to my gut being triggered in some way. There was no way to prove it and I simply had to accept it as my body told me that this wasn't good for me. Again, all fine now but I still avoid processed bread and eat sourdough instead.

Blood Sugar Issues

As I previously stated, controlling blood sugar was monumental for me during acute and well into the recovery stage. I was eating protein every two to three hours to stay on top of this as is recommended for diabetics managing insulin issues. Going past an hour or more from this regimen brought on extreme dizziness and panic attacks from feeling like I was going to pass out. It was much easier to stay ahead of this issue than rest after and try to recover as usually that would take hours. Many people claim carbohydrates cause symptoms like this and contribute to the dreaded akisthia (not yet discussed) but I did not see a direct correlation other than my protein intake needed to offset my carb intake to keep my blood sugar regulated. I have also learned from others that abruptly stopping all processed food and/or sugar during this state can also lead to waves and even worse, setbacks so please never cold-turkey anything that your body is dependent on. I could not tolerate caffeine and still can't but some people who drink it every day and cold turkey are in more withdrawal distress than just benzo hell so please use caution.

Do Not Consume Alcohol

Alcohol is technically not a liquid benzodiazepine, but it does act on the GABA sites in a similar way. I was drinking socially while on both Ativan and Klonopin with no understanding that it compounded its sedative effects. To be honest in the year of daily use of Klonopin I had started drinking more alcohol as it was helping me to stay calmer as tolerance set in. Needless to say, getting off alcohol is a must in order to heal efficiently as it is working on the GABA in much the same way. But again, do not cold-turkey drinking but instead find a way to gradually decrease your intake if you dependent on alcohol from long term daily use (much like tapering a benzodiazepine).

Ironically, Ativan is prescribed to people in acute alcohol withdrawals to avoid life-threatening seizures. That is a good use for benzos but the patient must then get off the benzo and not be prescribed long-term as we know what happens then (some of my clients have been down this road). Now here is the big warning about alcohol. We have yet to discuss kindling as a term that is a drastic de-regulation of GABA receptors due to either a reinstatement dose after a prolonged period of abstinence from the benzodiazepine or drinking a substantial amount of alcohol during the recovery stage of this.

Not all will get setback as badly as others and some (very few) may even be able to drink continuously during withdrawals but it is a well-known that alcohol can kindle the withdrawal symptoms such that benzo hell is revisited even after months and years of feeling healed. I am not pleased about this either as I am part of a community of drinkers and enjoyed my wine and beer but this is part of accepting the healing process. I now have a new passion for finding alcohol free beer as well as making mocktails with alcohol-free beverages. This is a huge and growing industry as well so why not be excited to be part of this community? However; my go-to drink to order at restaurants is still cranberry and seltzer (with a lime) as this will look like a drink and tastes great.

Medications, Supplements, and Herbs that Can Cause Setbacks

Just as I stated in the beginning of this book, much of this protocol to heal efficiently is about what not to do as to avoid setbacks. Setbacks can occur when the same GABA receptors are antagonized with a chemical or supplement and further down regulate. Ironically, this down regulation can occur from too much of the wrong activity too but I am focusing on what goes into the mouth for this chapter. I already detailed my setback from eating the wrong foods in excess but what I want to bring your attention to is a valuable and comprehensive list of medications, supplements, and herbs to avoid during and even after benzo hell. Reference D on my website has this direct link that is from the Benzo Information Coalition website.

Here are the medications, herbs, and supplements from that BIC reference that I have found (either by my experience, working with others and/or reading benzo warriors stories) that could cause you to have a reaction or setback if you are tapering or benzo injured. Please do your research and go carefully if you decide to try anything new. Keep a journal to note any rev ups in your symptoms.

Remember that what works for one can set another back in their recovery. Alcohol, anticonvulsants, baclofen, fluoroquinolone antibiotics, LDN or Low Dose Naltrexo, lidocaine, magnesium, oregano oil, penicillin, phenibut, progesterone and estrogen, saffron extract, soma, ashwagandha, chamomile, GABA supplements, kava, L-theanine, passion flower, skullcap, valerian, epinephrine (This is a big one as it is often used with Novocain in dentist offices to enhance the numbing affects – as for carbocaine instead), and marijuana (all forms including CBD and THC) work with the brain's GABA pathways in the same way as benzos. Some claim CBD and THC helps them. Please be careful if you decide to experiment here. Also included are NSAIDS, opiates, antidepressants, antipsychotics, caffeine, food additives, preservatives and dyes, hormones (such as testosterone), mood stabilizers, MSG, OTC pain killers, SNRIs, SSRIs, and stimulants.

It's not always clear why certain compounds can cause a reaction or setback in someone who has been injured by benzodiazepines, but two possible explanations are hypersensitivity of the nervous system and neurotoxicity (the ability of the drugs to damage the nervous system either functionally or structurally).

If you're benzo injured, do your research, and talk to your doctor before taking anything, whether prescribed or over the counter. One of the most important things you can do to avoid a setback is to weigh the risks of everything you put into your mouth.

Functional Medicine Approach

I can tell you that my experience with functional medicine while in tolerance and not knowing it was nothing short of a disaster. Had I understood that the reason my health was deteriorating then maybe I could have explained the need to go slow with my supplementation, but I didn't. I went to the functional medicine doctor while in the second year of tolerance to see if I could get help with my fatigue and aches. They looked into my eyes and did a blood test and offered some healing clay services (bentonite clay). When I went back to review my results and get their recommendations for supplements: I was told that I was in a highly distressed state of health and needed no less than fourteen supplements to take three times a day in varying doses. Well, my body simply could not handle that so after paying close to $500 and trying to do this regimen, I was worse off. I can now take supplements. I do feel benefits from them, but I still take them in moderation and not all at the same time. So here is my guideline for supplementation: After acute (when the only goal is just to survive), try a quarter (¼) of the therapeutic dose to see if you have a reaction or if it helps. I would do this for at least a week before trying to increase the dose.

Chemicals Are Everywhere

Lastly, I feel compelled to include my intolerance of any chemicals during acute and still now have difficulty with them. I had no idea how prevalent chemicals were in my life until benzo hell. The affect that cleaning chemicals/aroma had on my nervous system (and still to a degree) was complete chaos and caused physical and mental anguish. I am talking about things like AJAX or anything with bleach and even laundry detergent. I would get so nauseated by the smell that I would have to vacate where it was being used immediately like it was a life-or-death situation. It is not nearly as bad, but I still have to ask my kids to not wear body sprays if I am going to be in the car with them for a long period. My aunt explained that this intolerance is our brains reacting to protect us from more harm. I am not sure what it is but it is real as many other benzo warriors have documented the same phenomenon. But I listen to my body and protect myself when I need to go down the cleaning solution aisle at Walmart by covering up with my shirt or a mask. I use organic chemical free solutions for cleaning at home like water and vinegar. I am getting much better dealing with this issue but wanted to make sure you knew if are having the same problems.

Chemicals are everywhere. Just be careful to protect yourself in the especially in the early stages of recovery. One of my clients was doing well in getting into the recovery stage of his journey until the parking lot that surrounded his apartment building was repaved. The toxic fumes from the new tar set him back at least a month with akathisia and digestive returning to the Acute-like stage. His father dug deeper into what is used to seal the new pavement and found that the MSDS (Material Safety Data Sheet) had indeed toxic chemical that obviously his compromised brain-blood barrier was not able to filter out as readily as a normal person would be able to do.

Chapter 8
Upregulation of GABA Receptors with a Mindful Protocol

I am going to introduce the heart of this protocol to efficiently heal and get through benzo hell in this chapter. It starts with doing exactly what you may be trying to avoid by trying things to get around, under or over benzo hell instead of through it. When you are desperately seeking help to deal with symptoms, there is much more to be gained by accepting this distressing yet temporary state than trying to get immediate relief by doing or taking something else.

Being present with the nervousness, pain and/or other distress of withdrawals and not distracting with mindless activity that over stimulate the brain is the name of the game here. The protocol outlined using mindfulness to stay present doing intervals of an activity followed by rest. Mindfulness is a practiced skill concentrating on what you are doing or seeing without letting judgement, thought, or limiting beliefs dissuade you from focusing. With each iteration of using mindfulness followed by rest, the theory is that new growth (or neuron connections) in the brain encourage upregulation of the GABA receptors. As the recovery progresses, immersion in positive feelings can be uses to optimize the brain to prefer this state of being. This is not to be confused with relying on positive thinking to do the work that the body needs to do to stabilize.

If you are in acute withdrawals of benzo hell in which the only goal is to survive each minute, then know that this is not the time to actively try to upregulate the damaged GABA receptors. This stage will pass on its own and requires that you rest without judgment as much as possible. We have had some conflicting philosophies on dealing with acute in the coaching realm but I think with enough time for reflection, even the most avid "fight through this stage" warrior has recognized this stage for what it is. It is an injury that needs to be protected to heal. This chapter is about when you are transitioning and/or past this acute stage and are ready for the recovery Stage of benzo hell. Yes, you are still in benzo hell as the symptoms rage on with either waves and windows or a consistent baseline of suffering. That is why we call it benzo hell because the feeling that there is malice by the devil being done to us can be even worse than acute in that time seems to pause and we live each day in repetition of dreading these symptoms. My job with this book and my coaching is to make this recovery stage as efficient as possible so that you get through benzo hell.

Your Role in Recovery

Whether or not you prepared yourself for benzo hell with the radical acceptance of your injury or you are now in benzo hell just realizing the extent of the damage that prescribed long term benzodiazepines have done, now is the time to recognize that healing is going to take some effort by you. There is no way around, under, or over benzo hell but there is a way through it. Start the process of recovery wherever you are at and let go of previous expectations or judgements that may have been preventing you from healing. I told you that much of this protocol is about what not to do and this is exactly the worst time to be considering how we got into benzo hell with regret and/or remorse. Holding on to that fury is not going to help and if fact can impede healing. The positive shifts in your mindset that take place as you heal are predicated on being able move the needle in the right direction and not from ruminating on what you can't do. This mindset is developed as we retrain our thinking from being in survival mode to being in the recovery stages.

Transitioning out of Acute into Recovery Stage

While in the acute stage of benzo hell, the brain is operating in a survival mode while the symptoms are consuming our thoughts. There doesn't seem to be room in our thought process to think as all the focus is on the symptoms. This was quite apparent in my story in Chapter 2 as I knew how to unload the dishwasher but was unable to figure out how to physically do it. A door must be opened – just a crack to let the light into that dark place in our head. That light is going to be your belief in healing. How can I suggest that you think that you can believe that you can heal when you can't even process time? I can tell you what my aunt told me. This injury needed to be protected in acute so those symptoms that prevented us from doing anything except for surviving were helping us to heal. Even though this is an invisible injury, it is like any other physical injury that requires extreme caution to prevent it from making it worse. That door needs to be opened by you and effort needs to take place in the form of movement. The belief that you can heal comes from understanding that progress is made by simply setting an intention. It is not by seeing immediate results. Trusting that her process was going to work due the fact that she is my aunt who was both knowledgeable and trustworthy, I believed that I was going to heal and that initiated my healing. This book is providing that knowledge as I guide you on to accelerating your recovery.

Get Off the Computer

The protocol started by getting off the computer which had been to that point my only connection to the "real" world. I continued to support others on BenzoBuddies.org but that time was limited as mindful activities were introduced and then eventually replaced the desire to search the internet for answers. The act of answer shopping was interfering with me trusting her process as well as overstimulating my brain. What I also learned from the Andrew Huberman podcast is that the eyes are unshielded parts of the brain and by getting direct visual stimulation was like assaulting the initial injury. Not only that, but the ability also to process the information that I was getting online was using up the reserve energy that I needed to focus on the mindful activity. I could immediately feel the difference by limiting the computer screen time even though I had only been doing it in bits of time for what I thought was helping me to be less isolated.

The truth was that after I had been validated with how benzodiazepines caused this massive breakdown of my health, I was obsessed with finding more information and digging myself deeper into fits of rage. What I had to be forced to remember after lying in bed for over a month doing nothing, but internet surfing is that "real" life is not reading or typing on the computer but doing real things. Another good reason to "unplug" and was mentioned in the article theorizing why chronic illness can result from prescribed long term benzodiazepine use is that the cycle producing the toxins could be in part perpetuated by EMI noise. I am not recommending that you put tinfoil around your bedroom to insulate you electromagnetic interference or fields, but I am politely suggesting that the farther away you can get from such networks and devices, the better set-up for your healing could be possible.

Mindfulness Activities

My aunt gave me small tasks to do that had nothing to do with the finished product but instead was about the process of doing it. The goal in doing something with my hands that would not physically exert me was to stay present with my thinking while I was doing the activity. This is called mindful activities. My state as I was coming out of benzo hell was that I felt I "should" be able to help around the house and be preparing food for the family. I wasn't ready at the beginning stages, but it is good to point out that these tasks did eventually turn into being able to contribute to the house but first I had to learn how to do it the right way. The intention of staying present would be set and then without judging my fleeting inability to stay focused on what I was doing, be active for five minutes doing that task with as much awareness as possible.

It is crucial that this mindful activity not be anything too mentally taxing as well as not pushing any physical limits in the beginning. I was mostly bed-ridden at this point and my hands would go numb if I lifted them for too long, so my initial activity was simply passing a tennis ball from one hand to the next. This was a task modified from something I had done as a child when I used to toss the ball up and catch it from a lying down position. I could not even fathom being able to do that activity requiring coordination and depth perception in acute but enjoyed the familiarity of the tennis ball in my hand as I squeezed, positioned, and then handed and eventually tossed the ball back and forth. Don Killian had tied and retied knots in a long rope as his mindful activity. One of my clients used four Legos and snapped them in different ways as the entry activity, another had a football that he loved and pretended to hike it from a seated position.

The Distinction Between Mindful Activities and Distraction

To be clear about the difference between mindful activities and distraction, we are not doing the mindful activity for entertainment or to momentarily feel better. Although this may result it is entirely different when your brain earns the feel-good feeling rather than it being served up to your body in the immediate gratification of hitting the dopamine receptors. Watching TV, going for a joy ride in the car, blaring music, surfing social media and other such activities are not mindful activities. Reading a book is a mindful activity (if it is possible and doesn't cause immediate pain depending on your cognitive abilities). This must be the most difficult thing to explain to people of earlier generations as they have a tendency that anything that brings them pleasure (legally) is up for grabs to use in this protocol. It is not. The mindful activity that I am referring to that helps upregulates the GABA receptors are not distractions.

Flow and Mindful Stepping

There is a state called "flow" that can be achieved when your thoughts and actions are truly engaged and keeping track of time fades away. Flow has been shown to be the optimal state of learning. We are not going to try to achieve flow with our mindful activities right away nor are we going to chase that state as it must come naturally. But what I am hoping is that you allow yourself to become entirely open to this state by being present and aware while concentrating on the mindful activity. I have been able to achieve this state in my recovery as I practiced having my attention fully on the activity. Being in this state of flow reminded me of building sandcastles on the beach as a child and that was when I felt myself coming back from the depths of benzo hell.

This state can be achieved through simple observation of a task being done (like watching ants build their ant hill) or even by watching the leaves on a tree blow with the wind. I can now achieve flow quite easily when watching the waves crash on the beach but please know that this wasn't even close to being possible in acute as the ocean (even though I grew up on the beach) scared me. The easiest way that I was able to induce this state of flow was through mindful stepping. This is when you synchronize the contact that your foot makes on the ground with counting numbers or saying the alphabet with letters such that you stay present with each step. I was able to start doing mindful stepping at month three when the tortuous bone aches were giving me breaks. I would gently walk in my backyard and would whisper knowing that I looked strange but let go of the judgement in doing this to get the results. This is when the uneven ground would cause my walking gait to be unsteady as well, so it wasn't a pretty sight. Mindful stepping for me now has evolved into looking for stumps and vines on the path in the woods where I walk at a fast pace to ensure that I am not going to trip on something. That is how this recovery evolves, with literal baby steps. But my point is that by "moving the needle" and doing mindful activity with intentions while not being concerned with limitations is how you start the process that will eventually lead to your recovery.

Active Resting as Integration (Optimizing Neuroplasticity)

The assessment of how I felt after a mindful activity didn't take place until I had actively rested for an equal or longer period of time. Actively resting sounds like an oxymoron as resting means relaxing and not being active. But what I would learn from my aunt is that the body and brain is integrating the activity that has been done while it is at rest. Again, it is the intention of relaxing with rest and not necessarily the ability to do this that matters. Whether you are sitting, reclining or lying down to rest, the posture that produces the most gains for your nervous system to integrate the activity is to actively open and expose your chest. This can be accomplished by keeping your hands by your sides and turning your facing up. It may feel more comfortable to have your body closed down like in a fetal position or with your hands curled up by your face but with slow practice, the ability to uncoil yourself and have your body in a relaxed state while keeping your chest exposed will become easier.

My aunt encouraged me in her authoritative way to not immediately scan my body for symptoms as soon as the activity was complete. Rather to keep the focus on the breath which is also hard to do in acute as the throat is often constricted. But by subjecting myself to her commands as she was not going to listen to excuses of why I couldn't do this, I did exactly as I was told and became aware of what this term integration means. The time following a mindful activity is when the new neural connections are solidified such that doing the task becomes much more natural and not difficult to repeat as our nervous system readjusts how it handles such stimulation.

I understand intervals of resting when you are already either bed-ridden or extremely limited could appear to be a waste of time but just as I learned by doing this, you will feel your body making these connections and becoming more regulated during rest intervals after the mindful activity. I still use resting as a means of integrating new activities. When returning to my old lifestyle activities (with a new mindset), I make sure to rest after the introduction before continuing to the next event as a means of integrating progress that I have made. I also protect my progress with intervals of rest as my daily activities become more fluent and demanding. I will address this more in documenting windows and waves but please understand that no matter what mindful activity you are doing and for whatever amount of time that the real work for our injury to heal comes during the rest period (integration) and not waste your efforts by skipping this part. And to be sure, the ultimate reward of active resting is sleep so please do not have any concerns if that is the result. Sleep after active resting doesn't need to be the objective for this protocol to work but it is a benefit for sure for those of us who have suffered without it for so long in tolerance and acute.

Moving the Needle with Mindful Activity

Once my attention of moving the ball back and forth was not interrupted by intrusive thoughts for the initial five minutes and I was able to successfully rest without my symptoms ramping up, it was time to start "moving the needle" again. If I tell you that passing a ball between two hands is exhausting and you don't believe me then you have not been in benzo hell as deep as I have and I am happy for that. But that was my entry into mindful activity. You can find your starting point by finding an activity that interests you and/or brings you some calmness while staying focused on the process of doing it. It is important that your starting point is not a productive task but one that you select as a process for this entry due to how that intention affects the outcome. Please understand that I was not relearning how to do tasks, but I was teaching my brain that it could handle other than operating in that survival mode.

My aunt would later recommend higher executive function tasks that had a productive outcome but before then I was moved on to other activities that had once been an interest to me while I was growing up but long forgotten due to life and being sedated. These activities included building towers with building blocks (I used Jenga blocks), coloring in an adult coloring book, practicing my calligraphy, observing nature (more on that later), and other immature sounding tasks. How I knew that I was ready to start more complex tasks without risking being overstimulated was my call to make but she encouraged me to keep moving forward. Her reminders of what I had successfully done turned into me tracking my accomplishments in my journal as my progress continued. I encourage my clients to do the same as keeping track of what they have been able to do helps to offset the disappointment of what they cannot do during this stage of benzo hell.

You can find your starting point by finding an activity that interests you and/or brings you some calmness while staying focused on the process of doing it. It is important that your starting point is not a productive task but one that you select as a process for this entry due to how that intention affects the outcome. Please understand that I was not relearning how to do tasks, but I was teaching my brain that it could handle other than operating in that survival mode. The time frame in which increasing these activities into chores was about two months from beginning to end which was encouraging to me after I had been unable to do much of anything for the first two and half months. Your time frame will be different as I have explained so try not to despair or compare.

Measurable Progress, Duty Cycle, and the Law of Diminishing Returns

The measurable progress in the recovery stage is not how long you can sustain a mindful activity but how often you can do that activity again with repeated success. This time interval is called a duty cycle in automation and is a percentage of time on verse time off. A motor running at 50 percent duty cycle is operating half the time while dormant half the time. The operation in this case is someone is doing an activity versus resting (this includes active resting and sleeping). A duty cycle of 100 percent is continuous operation or doing an activity all day long while a dusty cycle of 0 percent is resting all day. I was limited in how long I could do anything due to exhaustion and needed to rest often but I thought (until otherwise educated) that if I was able to do the activity for longer periods of time then I was getting better. I was wrong. The protocol for healing this injury is such that any activity during recovery is consistently limited to a maximum set time which in my case was five minutes at first then building up to thirty minutes. That hard stop for the time period was kept consistent, so that once I had achieved ten minutes of folding laundry but had not successfully rested without symptoms, I would go back to that limit of ten minutes until I completed the cycle with repeated success.

Having this time limit doesn't mean that the complexity or intensity of the task can't be increased as you progress but there is a law of diminishing returns when it comes to doing too much for too long in the recovery stage. The induced state of "flow" is wonderful to achieve while doing a mindful activity, but we still have to treat ourselves carefully as doing too much can cause overstimulation to our developing brain connections. Also, having a time limit on the active period interval is a way to keep the intention whatever we are doing to be about healing even while doing productive tasks.

Again, this was a new way of thinking for me as I looked at tasks in my old life as things to accomplish and my success was based on how quickly I could complete them. This book is being written to get you through benzo hell so that you may return to daily living as normal but in order to get there, this is the iterative protocol for efficient healing. The duty cycle of your mindful activities increases by how quickly your body recovers from the activity and can do this again. This also applies to external stimulation in that your body is seeing and experiencing needs to be limited with equal amounts of rest until your nervous system has the resiliency to handle long term exposure. As we get back to living more normal lives after getting through benzo hell, the duty cycle of how often we are doing tasks is going to naturally increase.

Breathwork to Help Mindfulness

I had many symptoms (understatement as it was probably close to fifty different symptoms) in acute, but I specifically documented air hunger as being one of the primary ones due to how completely distressing it was. I was obviously breathing but my autonomic system had been disrupted by the injury such that I felt that I was either not inhaling frequently enough or over inhaling causing hyperventilation. What I found to work was not focusing on the inhaling but drawing my attention to expanding my lower rib cage and stomach when I inhaled. So instead of breathing being an upper operation by the lungs, the body (diaphragm) is bringing the air deep down where the oxygen can saturate into the bloodstream, and you feel the satisfaction. I would do this for a few breaths and then be able to breathe normally until I needed to do it again. This technique is the opposite of feeling like you are just "sipping the air." Just because this technique helped me doesn't necessarily mean that it should help you so if trying this causes more angst then simply let the suggestion go. I would later learn about box breathing which is a four-part cycle of doing a controlled inhale, hold, exhale, hold before inhaling again for four seconds each. That was also helpful to do a few times to re-establish normal breathing. A few times is key; this is not something that you do continuously.

Further along in the recovery stage and as an added benefit, I found breathwork to be an even greater tool in both staying present as well as calming my nervous system down when it was overstimulated. There are plenty of people on YouTube and even phone applications to teach you about breathwork if you Google Breathwork for Anxiety. We can use these methods of activating our sympathetic nervous system for healing but remember that our goal is to "move the needle" and not do anything to an extreme. There are some dangerous types of breathing techniques to avoid so keep the investigation into using this tool controlling anxiety and not for releasing trauma or achieving an altered state. Having said all that, I brought the breathwork up in the context of using it to stay present doing the mindful activity and rest for another reason. When your breathing is regulated on its own and you no longer feel like you are fighting for air as a daily battle, I encourage you to try to breathe just through your nose if possible. I do realize that sinus congestion, which is also a symptom in benzo hell, may limit your ability to do this so don't worry if you can't. But there are benefits from breathing through your nose that include the formation of nitric oxide on the exhale which improves oxygen circulation and makes you feel calmer. Nose breathing is not imperative for the mindful activity to be successful but can help optimize what the protocol is intending to do.

Remember That This Is a Nonlinear Healing Process and What Not to Do in Windows

It is crucial to reiterate that this is not a linear healing process and therefore the duty cycle of how often I was doing something needed to be adjusted and still does based on how I am feeling. Yes, that means that the duty cycle of how often you do your mindful activity (that may have progressed to actual productive chores) may need to decrease based on intensity of symptoms. Nothing is lost in terms of gains in your recovery when having to scale back rather you will be protecting yourself for lowering the duty cycle as needed. What proves that this protocol in working and that forward progress is being made is that your ability to do the task within that defined period isn't lost. For example, I could not make my bed to save my life in acute due to fatigue, muscle tension and head pressure. But by slowly building up to this complex task, I made my bed even when that was the only mindful activity I could do for that day before resting.

When supporting clients, I try to re-assure them that this is not a structured protocol based but is based on where they are in that stage in their recovery. The nonlinear part of the recovery is how the brain heals but often people find out the hard way that pushing past their limits will induce waves. I simply can't convince everyone from over-doing it until they learned that lesson themselves as was with the case of my client Walter. This older man is an over-achiever by nature and with a productive work ethic. He sent me YouTube video of himself playing music and I was astounded at how young and vibrant he was for his age. We started working together at the end of his taper off Valium (he had crossed over from Klonopin) and he was feeling the symptoms of benzo hell. I had a great time getting to know him and his wife while he was feeling a bit better upon cessation of the medication, and it was obvious that they are a great team together. But as he felt much better in Week five after the jump, he abandoned the protocol of doing a mindful activity followed by rest and started painting all the trim on his house as project. He did this for three days straight and even had a beer. Then he spent the next two months doubting that he would ever heal and in misery with acute-like symptoms. It was back to the basics with him, and he is now slowly regaining his ability to do more things and has learned from this experience.

This is not a complicated protocol to apply if you recognize that the structure of limiting your activities is protecting you from waves and setbacks.

Being able to complete and repeat a mindful activity successfully is the objective but then having a day or week or even month when the assessment after resting indicates that you are in more distress is just part of the nonlinear healing. Accepting that it is time to rest more and not increase the duty cycle of the activities is just as important as moving the needle with starting the mindful activities intervals. You can find your starting point by finding an activity that interests you and/or brings you some calmness while staying focused on the process of doing it. It is important that your starting point is not a productive task but one that you select as a process for this entry due to how that intention affects the outcome. We are actively upregulating our GABA receptors by being mindful that the process has only one objective and that is to heal us. Multi-tasking the exact opposite of what is being promoted in this protocol. In fact, as you become aware of your healing process and start recognizing windows and waves; it is imperative that we don't use a window to break the protocol and do more than what is being outlined or risk being set back due to overstimulation. Our brains are not going to heal faster by trying to be productive before we have mastered being mindful.

Imagery

By getting a clear picture in our heads of what is happening during healing this iatrogenic injury, you can accelerate your body's ability to heal. I know that imagining anything in the early stages of recovery can be difficult due to our compromised cognitive abilities but I will explain why imagery is worth spending some time cultivating. Imagery in this context is mentally visualizing something happening that you can't see or do at that time (but may want to do in the future). Dr. Joe Dispenza is the foremost expert on the brain and body connections in healing by both education, practice and healing himself from a severe back injury through visualization. He happened to be a chiropractor, so he knew the mechanics of the spine and what had been damaged in his cycling accident. What he did was he systematically focused on each part of his back that needed to be healed and visualized how the healing was taking place. My experience using imagery when I was playing competitive sports allowed me to grasp this concept of imagining your body making something happen much easier, but I still struggled with the abstract part of this brain injury which we cannot see.

I am certainly not saying that we can upregulate our GABA receptors by using imagery alone, but I believe that it helps as I will explain how I applied this. My image that I used to create a visual of this healing process was that the GABA receptors were long blades of grass in a field. The soil has provided the perfect nutrients for this grass to grow, and it is healthy and flowing but some of it has been tramped down to lie flat on the ground by a farm tractor. With sun, water and fresh air; that grass will slowly come back to a vertical position. As the symptoms become intense is when that trampled grass is doing its best to get back to being vertical as it takes work. My job is to protect that grass and give it all the water and sun (not too much) that it needs to successfully become part of the field of tall standing grass. Upregulating the GABA receptors so that they can receive the chloride ions to inhibit the over excitatory state of having too much Gluatamate is what will calm our central nervous system. We have the capacity to do this and the imagery is just helping facilitate the efficiency of getting it done.

Grounding and Immersion in Nature

No matter what stage you are in benzo hell, I highly encourage you to make going outside in bare feet (if possible) and standing directly on the ground a daily habit (if possible, with temperature and your capabilities). If you can walk around with your shoes off, then even better. To understand why I recommend doing this as part of the protocol let's refer to the only study that provides a hypothesis for how benzo withdrawals can manifest into chronic illness. Recall that the ion channels that allow the excitatory neurons could be stuck open due to the voltage potential between neurotransmitters and receivers. The excess of excitatory neurons is what is referred to as the glutamate storm and that is how it feels as our bodies are inflamed and highly reactive. My interpretation was lowering that voltage potential that would allow those channels to close and thereby reach homeostasis. The literal ground is a means of closing those channels by minimizing the voltage potential in our cells. In electrical circuits, a ground is when the voltage is brought to its lowest potential and inhibits the current to flow.

Our bodies are full of electrical energy so by putting our bare feet on the ground, we are helping to reduce how readily our synapse between neurotransmitter and receivers respond. There are YouTube videos by other benzo warriors who claim that sitting by a tree on the ground can calm the nervous system as well or even better than the benzos did and with lasting effects. I know that when I immerse myself in nature by simply going outside (not in acute) that there is a calming effect that feels like I am more grounded. I do have to warn of the effects of direct sunlight here though as it literally felt like the sun was like kryptonite to Superman. I would literally feel the sun burning my skin and would immediately become exhausted but later found out that this symptom was in fact my body protecting me. UV Light is shown to lower BH4 which the same study concluded leads to more oxidative stress.

Typical Life Now that Includes Mindfulness

My typical day at four years after abrupt cessation of benzos still includes this protocol of mindfulness and intervals of activity but my duty cycle of being able to more and more is still increasing as I heal. I am up and productive for about 80 percent of the day but my definition of being productive also includes energy that I spend time doing a mindful activity for myself which is also called self-care. I take gentle walks in nature to offset the natural chaos of family life. I often rest after going grocery shopping due to the added stimulation of the lights (more on that in next chapter). I will go out to a social event after preparing myself with alone time before to preserve my energy. I travel to Colorado every few weeks in the winter and I take a couple of days to rest when I arrive.

But it is the day-to-day chores of cooking, cleaning and doing assembly work for our family business that allow me to practice mindfulness now that I am back to a normal life. I feel the water as I rinse the plates, I bend to load the dishwasher and have gratitude that my joints do not scream in pain, I organize the dishes so that space is optimized without rushing to complete the task and I remember to breathe using my diaphragm so that remain calm and present. It is not a chore but a ritual that grounds me as I remember that panicked feeling when I was in acute and just stared at the dishwasher without having the capability to do anything. I am not saying that all tasks become enjoyable as picking dog poop is still not something to look forward to but I am living my life with a new appreciation for all that I can do rather than lamenting on what I can't do. That is healing to me.

Chapter 9
Help Dealing with Physical Symptoms

If I could do one thing with this book that would help you get through benzo hell, it would be to validate all your physical symptoms no matter what they are. The body and brain are literally rebuilding their nervous system after long-term prescribed use of benzodiazepines, and it is painful to say the least. While the validation doesn't alleviate the symptoms, it does make dealing with the suffering easier. Without this validation, the mind gets "stuck" into believing that this pain will never end and/or thinking that this is a new neurological disease that needs treatment. The reason why I think validating your symptoms as being in benzo hell is so important is so that you don't seek that medical intervention that can worsen the condition be treated as well as prolong recovery. This chapter can't possibly address each and every bizarre physical symptom (there are well over 100 documented) but validation helped and is helping everyone who I have ever known to get though benzo hell. I am going say with 99 percent degree of confidence that if you didn't have the physical sensation, pain or difficulty before benzo then it is just a symptom and not some ailment that needs medical attention in order to go away. I am not a medical doctor and do not have any skin in wanting to minimize your symptoms, but I have found that the cold, hard truth that physical pain is part of getting through benzo hell.

To further and more professionally validate the specific symptoms that I address, please Reference R in the resources on my website for a comprehensive list generated by the The Alliance for Benzodiazepine Best Practices. They refer to these as typical benzodiazepine withdrawal syndrome symptoms. While I have categorized this as being in benzo hell, D.E. Foster introduced the term BIND in the recorded live presentation by benzo warrior which is referenced as S under my resources. BIND stands for Benzodiazepine Induced Neurological

Dysfunction. It is defined as a constellation of functionally limiting neurological symptoms (both physical and psychological) that are the consequences of neuroadaptation and/or neurotoxicity to benzodiazepine exposure. Remember that acute is the stage in which surviving is the only objective and you do whatever you can to just hold on minute to minute, hour to hour. Know that this is a temporary state. What I am addressing is the dealing with physical symptoms after the acute stage.

Rigid Muscles and Locked Joints

Everyone has their own worst symptoms in benzo hell and rigid muscles with locked joints was mine. My body was like a board that couldn't bend. Had I not known that this was a neurological injury manifesting in ways that are not dependent on the condition of the body then I would have surely believed and sought treatment for the most progressive form of arthritis that could be possible. And I am sure that inflammation markers in my blood would have confirmed such a degenerative disease. I even posted on BenzoBuddies.org about not being able to wipe myself after going to the bathroom due to my shoulders being locked up. Yes, I am LeslieJ. Now I can walk, hike and garden as well as work out with my personal trainer without any pain (most of the time).

The Ashton Manual has a passage on this in Chapter 3 that I must have read a thousand times and held on dearly to the hope that I would be released from this vice that locked my hips, SI joint and rib cage. "There are many measures that will alleviate these symptoms, such as muscle stretching exercises as taught in most gyms, moderate exercise, hot baths, massage and general relaxation exercises. Such measures may give only temporary relief at first, but if practiced regularly can speed the recovery of normal muscle tone – which will eventually occur spontaneously." – Ashton Manual; Reference A on my website. There was never a spontaneous release of this rigidity for me, but I certainly was able to get bits of relief that showed that indeed what she had documented was happening.

Moving the Needle with Gentle Movement to Encourage Muscle Release

After I got out of acute (when all I could do was simply pray for the release of my muscles), my aunt (occupational therapist) helped me with specific movements to encourage the joint to release as part of the mindful protocol with activity followed by rest. Those movements started with simple pelvic tilts in bed and progressed to sitting on a yoga ball and using my torso to "draw" letters. I can't even write about this without feeling the desperation of not being able to move freely and each movement bringing pain. I did myself no favors by constantly digging into my sides with my fingers to release the rigidity as I will share more about soon. The biggest gains in this arena of my recovery came from having small windows open after doing gentle movement. A client who had not experienced any windows after four months from jumping was able to do some Thai Chi practice that they had done years before and with small mindful movements. She was overjoyed with her first window as her symptoms relented following the period of rest after. Encouraging the body to open and move with the intention being healing instead of recovery or judgement of physical limitations is going to move the needle to regaining flexibility and strength. It may not happen right away for you like it did for her but your belief that relief is obtainable will certainly get you closer to achieving this.

A Scary Story to Learn From

I became close with a few people on BenzoBuddies.org offline and we shared many tragic stories about how benzos had ruined our lives (up until being able to heal). One such friend was an avid mountain bike rider. She had been in phenomenal shape when she was put in benzo hell and it made it even more devastating that she was bedridden with much of the same systems that I had. She had been working for a few weeks after she finally got out of acute on rebuilding her muscle strength and stamina (slowly) when a window opened. She felt the amazing feeling of being healed and I can attest from experience how enticing this opportunity to do stuff that you love is at this time. She went on a seven-mile bike ride in the desert heat with some friends and ended up back in a wheelchair for four more months. This is an extreme testament of what not to do but my point is that most of us have what is called exercise intolerance in benzo hell and it is not something to push through even in a window.

Healing with Gentle Massage by Someone Who Understands

I had the most healing experience that I could have ever hoped for about three weeks after I came home from my detox. I was still bed-ridden and needed assistance with everything at that time. My husband and I had been using a massage therapist over many years as we are both active in sports and he brought me to see her. I had to cover up in the car and arrived shaking and barely able to talk. I was sure I was going to pass out. She looked at me and asked him what was going on. She immediately understood my state even if she was in total disbelief that it had already been three weeks since my detox (she thought it was more like days due to how bad I was). Her brother had been through street drug withdrawals, and she recognized the symptoms.

I undressed in front of her, and she let out a yelp when she saw the bruising that I had created by trying to release my muscles with my hands by pounding on my body. She settled down, and with her help, I got onto the massage table, and her service became an experience of love and healing as her hands moved gently, and her voice re-assured me that I would survive. She used lavender oil on a tissue near my nose and it calmed me in a way that I didn't know possible. I continue to use diluted lavender oil for the rest of my recovery. It was not a massage where she attempted to release my muscles through pressure points but a more a gentle surface touching that made me feel safe and allowed my stiffness to release. It was not an easy trip and I didn't return until two weeks later but I think it was a turning point for me to know that someone could help me with some of this horrible pain. I had only used massage previously as a way to help optimize my flexibility and reduce soreness, so this type of healing massage was yet another transformation of my thinking of self-care.

Pins in Joints Continue in Waves

After the rigidity and locked joints receded, I was met with a new symptom that many benzo warriors are familiar with. I call it having "pins in my joints" because that is exactly what it feels like. I can move and flex my joints but there is a hitching with a sharp pain as my hips, elbows and neck feel like there are tiny pins getting in the way of the joint movement. It isn't something that anyone can understand unless they have felt it but I know many of us have had it from my research and talking with others. Some didn't even know it was a real symptom until I spoke up on-line but were highly appreciative of being validated that it does exist.

The strangest part is that these pin sensations come and go in windows and waves but the person experiencing them can forget that they went away and begin to believe that it is a permanent condition. I am talking about this from experience as well as literally identifying this symptom with someone who will later deny that they have this issue only to remember when it returns and then forget that it was gone. So bizarre but I think it has to do with our brains wanting to dismiss the suffering from our memories while also fearing that the suffering is real and will never go away. I still get this symptom when in Waves and know exactly what to do to minimize its intensity and duration (which includes a lot of rest) and more importantly what not to do.

What I have left from all this trauma to my joints and muscles is something called crepsis. Crepsis is a painless crackling of the joints when moving and I have it primarily in my hips. People can hear it when they climb stairs next to me. I am almost fifty years old and played competitive sports most of my life so it could be from that as well, but I am pretty sure that I would not have this to the degree that I have if I had not been through benzo hell. My primary advice for those in recovery mode is to keep moving with gentle intentions in a low impact manner. I have had plenty of conversation with past runners who insist that running helps them to feel better only to find out that they are suffering with this crepsis even more than I am. As with everything else that I learned on this journey, I was not the type of person who would choose to do yoga over going for a run for exercise but now I value that my body needs safe guided movement instead of intense physical activity.

Deep Bone Aches and Neuropathy

I didn't know what it was, but my butt was killing me in acute. It was like the circulation was cut off to my glutes and then the pain of getting the blood back was excruciating. Then I felt like cold and hot water was being poured down my shins. The bottoms of my feet would prickle with pins and needles and my hands would be ice cold and numb. And the absolute most horrendous type of deep aches in my upper thighs like my bones had cavities and were rotting. Some benzo warriors have burning spines in benzo hell which I did not have as a symptom, but I can only imagine how horrific that feels. All of this is referred to as Neuropathy which is damage or dysfunction of the nerves. As we understand that our neurotransmitters have been affected throughout our whole peripheral nervous system, the pieces come together to explain how such bizarre symptoms could possibly be related to this little pill called a Benzo.

What I recommend in dealing with all these symptoms is to not chase them by going to the doctor unless you feel like your life is in danger. I am sure that my hands shaking was a sign of Parkinson's and now they are completely stable without any issues at all. The strength in my grip has returned such that I can grab an eight pack of seltzers with one hand while I used to struggle to put a gallon of milk away with two hands. Ice, heat and then as I was able to tolerate Ibuprofen combined with Tylenol were helpful in dealing with these symptoms along with of course rest. I also found that a weighted blanket on my legs provided comfort which confirms the neurological aspect of this physical pain. Unfortunately, many people get prescribed Gabapentin during this period of benzo hell to deal with the Neuropathy and then just end up dependent on that medication with its own withdrawals. I also fear that many people are diagnosed with a list of illnesses presented in the first Chapter and either get put on more medication and/or accept this way of life as their new identity.

CBD Oil for Me

I do have to go out on a precarious branch here and say that CBD oil (Manufacturer: Charlotte Web) did in fact alleviate my deep bone pain temporarily. I was extremely grateful to my husband for suggesting it one night in my fourth month when I was still struggling to stand and do the dishes. I hesitated and then just said so be it if it makes me worse and was ready to accept that consequences. Ten minutes after taking it; my bone aches diminished to barely being there and I could stand without trembling. It was short lived though, and I refused to become dependent on another form of medication even it was natural. I still use CBD oil two to three times a week and in waves but I am well aware that it does not work in acute and others have had negative effects from using it. All I can say is that it is not a cure but a tool that I found that helps me.

Beliefs are a strong influencer in how we feel. If you believe that you are chronically ill rather than having a temporary benzo withdrawal symptom, then the outcome could be making how you feel worse. I know how awful you feel in benzo hell. Please try to accept this is a necessary and temporary state in our recovery so that healing is complete. You are not tragically ill for life. Your nerves are reconnecting, and it is painful. The most frustrating part is not being able to give you a timeline on healing. I have tried to come up with an algorithm for predicting when someone will be through benzo hell based on the dosage and years on the medication, but it is impossible due the fact that there are so many other variables. But this resource is giving you the knowledge to heal as efficiently as possible.

Lifestyle Choices in Recovery Affect Healing and Listening to Your Body

Our lifestyle choices are the primary ways in which we either heal efficiently or not at all. Continuing to go to the gym and lifting heavy weights after going to the tanning booth will not be conducive to healing as my good friend is showing me even though he eats a superbly nutritious diet and is in impeccable shape. We all have decisions to make during this process and like him, some of us may choose to do what we love regardless of how it affects our healing and that is totally our prerogative, but I am a benzo recovery health coach and will advise against anything that contributes to overstimulating the nervous system during the recovery stage. Period. I love my dear friend and hope he isn't going to hate me after reading this. Another important thing to do is be aware of when your body is telling you to rest or that you are pushing it too much. Bee stings on my lips were a clear indication when I was pushing it too much beyond what my nervous system could handle and would soon suffer if I didn't slow down.

The Dreaded Akathisia

Being unable to sit still while all these symptoms are raging is a whole other depth of benzo hell. If you have done any YouTube diving about benzo withdrawals, then you have undoubtedly seen the horror of akathisia shown by brave benzo warriors who are moving in constant motion. I had only experienced a form of this at night when I would literally be "swimming" in my bed unable to stop my legs and arms from moving due to an impossibly restless state. That was horrendous enough. That symptom for me would rage back after something like traveling by bus, plane and car all in one day to make the trip from NH to Colorado as I do many times of year. But the people who urgently move around for hours and seem to be "cattle-prodded" to do so are in the worst misery have my utmost compassion.

It is a cruel and dehumanizing symptom that caused even the great psychologist Jordan Peterson to seek refuge from being put in a coma in Russia. I am not going to diverge here yet, but he has yet to recognize that his suffering (admittedly from abruptly discontinuing prescribed long-term benzodiazepines) was so painful both mentally and physically that even he, with all his money, noted success being famous and education, could not find relief from this dreaded symptom. How he survived was with the help of his daughter and son-in-law being relentless in seeking ways to get him through this ordeal and that, not medical help, is what probably saved him. This act of trying to find ways to survive the symptoms keeps hope alive and ends up turning into healing in the end. So, if you are currently suffering from akathisia, then please is be curious about what helps and what makes this symptom worse. It will pass with time but your job is to actively note and apply these things that contribute to its dampening or revving up of the need to move. My client Jason felt a direct correlation from eating processed foods and his akathisia escalating, and I witnessed this to be true through real-time Face Time calls.

Akathisia and Preserving Windows

Some of the same benzo warriors are also videoing themselves in the throes of awful akathisia are also showing themselves going for late night joy rides when their symptoms subside briefly in windows only to come back with full symptoms again after doing such. In all my counseling of people in benzo hell I have noticed a significant quandary that makes the difference in healing. People will open the call with how bad they are doing and proceed to tell me that they were feeling better so that they did some amazing fun things and list the exciting ventures as a good thing that they accomplished. I want people to be healthy and happy but hearing that they lived the life that they were living before this mess with no regard how it affects their future sustained recovery even after I have educated them on the protocol to heal makes me think that I am just spinning my wheels for nothing. However, if they learn from their mistakes and accept that they have overdone something and that this is not how we heal efficiently then I gladly validate their mistake and help them find ways to get back to basic of self-care and resting. There will be plenty of opportunities to step back into what you used to do if you decide that is what you want to do but please know that during the recovery time and especially if you are suffering from akathisia that now is not the time to attempt to go back to living your old life that led to the need for benzodiazepines.

Skin, Hair, and Fingernails

I looked in the mirror and saw a much older person staring back at about three months after my rapid detox. I hadn't been able to see myself until then nor did I have the energy to care but slowly I was becoming more aware of how this terrible injury had aged me. My skin was loose, and my eyes looked hollow due to purple circles around them. I had noticed that there were deep horizontal lines on my fingernails, but it was later that I learned (as they grew out) that they were in fact indications of the trauma that my body had been through. I developed several skin issues in that the skin on my body was extremely dry while at the same time my hair was excessively oil which played into developing hyperplasia on my face (which would have to be treated professionally when I was much more recovered).

I had also noticed that clumps of hair would be left in my hands when rinsing in shower but hadn't had the energy to investigate further until this point. I saw that older person in the mirror with wrinkles, graying and thinning hair and thought I was a goner. More importantly, I thought how the hell do my kids see me when I am looking like this but didn't even realize it. I knew that they were informed about my condition and that I was obviously incapacitated most of the time, but I didn't know that I looked so ill in this dramatic moment of realization. It took a good year until my appearance returned to near normal as it can be in middle age but even my friends in my health coach classes began to ask what I was doing differently to look so much younger. I think the key to regaining some of my youthful appearance was by replenishing lost nutrients from prescribed long-term benzodiazepine use with whole foods.

As my recovery progressed into the second year, I did start to use skin products which I had never done before and now I am proud to say that I have a collection of serums and a micro needling kit. The reason that I am proud of this is that it shows that I care again and take my appearance seriously enough to invest in it. But I am in no way getting neurotoxin injections or a face lift for obvious reasons.

Ear, Eyes, Throat, and Teeth Pain

One of my first symptoms of withdrawals was deep ear pain as the time to take the second dose of the day approached. It would go away with that dose within minutes showing how dependent I was on benzodiazepines. That pain got immeasurably worse in acute and lingered for many months. The ear pain was accompanied by feeling like my ears had filled up with fluid as well. I even went to the ear doctor about having a possible ear infection to no avail as they were perfectly normal. That sensation still returns to a degree when I have pushed my body too much, so I use it another "indicator" for when it is time to slow down and be calm.

My throat was also sore and constricted much of the time. Many others report choking a bit with this symptom, and I can totally see how this could happen. I also had blurry vision that was not corrected with my normal eyeglasses. An uncomfortable visit to the eye doctor, in which I trembled the whole time, showed that my eyesight was not compromised but that the health of the tear ducts was causing severely dry eyes. That cleared up for me as well, but I still can't wear contacts for long and I used to wear them for twelve hours a day before benzo hell.

Phantom pains all over our bodies are normal in benzo hell as even our teeth sometimes feel infected or that they are falling out, but a dentist visit should alleviate that fear. If you can't get to the dentist, then I hope this helps validate your pain without you needing to be in crisis to get to the dentist for confirmation. But as with all these symptoms, it is better to be checked out medically if you have a real concern about your health than just write the pain off due to benzo withdrawals if there is a persistent problem. I just know that once we go looking for more medical interventions that we are now open to possible more iatrogenic injuries.

Hypnic Jerks

You may have had this falling sensation before when you are starting to fall asleep, and all a sudden, your body flails. These are called sleep starts but having such involuntary movements while totally awake are called hypnic jerks. They are the most bizarre reactions that I have ever felt in my body. I am a person who already doesn't like to be touched by others so it was doubly worse for me when someone would try to comfort me with an arm pat or some light pressure and my body would revolt in a spastic way. It would also happen without any instigation too. I have seen others on YouTube suffering with hypnic jerks and it looks like the person has a form of Tourette's when it is bad. I was alone for much of the time of benzo hell so this was not as big of an issue for me in terms of being embarrassed but I could much relate if a person had to be in public when this was happening and in fact have seen and recognized this symptom with others. I want to reach out to them (not touch them) and re-assure them that this is a transitional period when the nervous system is reregulating itself but who knows where they are in their journey (and they probably would not appreciate the insight). However, these hypnic jerks can also be a precursor to a seizure so if you are experiencing them soon after a cut or detox then please get this checked out with a medical professional immediately.

Head Pressure Galore

I could not put my head below my waist for almost two years without severe head pressure. I did not experience constant head pressure that whole time, but that position would bring it back within seconds. This is not just a tight band headache as previously discussed but an inner pressure that feels like your head is going to explode. A good indicator for when I was going to get this head pressure is when my shoulders tightened up. By the time I entered the recovery stage, heat and rest would often curtail the head pressure if paid attention to this tightness. I know for a fact that screens (laptop, phone, and such) made this symptom even worse but I also found that there was also a direct correlation to how long I on the screens the length of time that I would suffer after. For example: I could have never watched a movie in acute but watched half of the episode on Netflix at about nine months off. The content had to be as relaxing as possible (no violence). I would stop watching as soon as my shoulder started tightening up and could avoid the prolonged head pressure this way.

I gradually built up to being able to watch a whole Netflix series show by about a year until my twelve-month wave hit. During that wave I had to discontinue all use of screens for two months in order to protect myself I, of course, consulted my aunt who explained that the recovery that I had made wasn't lost but that I had to go back to being careful with my eyes and brain while adjustments were being made in the healing process of my injury. Acceptance was needed and well worth it as I am able to watch the news and shows now without issue as I make sure to not overdo it. That head pressure was just awful and I am hoping that you understand that it is a symptom that is telling you that rest is needed and there is no rationale for pushing through it yet. Be gentle with yourself.

Electrical Sensations and Grounding

There is an illustration that I wished I was able to share with you that a talented benzo warrior drew depicting what it feels like to be in benzo hell but I am not able to locate the person to reproduce it with their permission. It shows a person connected to a car battery with jumper cables and the obvious effect of being electrocuted. Sorry if that is a triggering visual. But this is exactly how I and many others feel in acute. The jolts of electricity that run from the brain to the feet and/or hands are torturous. Occasionally when overstimulated by too much of anything including sun, sounds, stress, these shocks can return in the recovery stage as a reminder that there in an injury to protect. I am sorry if you too are feeling such electrical sensations to any degree but know that this is indeed a physical symptom and not something that needs medical attention.

A big part of what I talk about on my Instagram account (@BenzoRecovery.JennyK) is how immersion in nature has helped me and many other benzo warriors with their recovery and to specifically deal with the excess of electrical activity that comes with healing. The sights, sounds, feel and even smell of a natural environment will help diffuse the electrical activity. One of my clients lived in the heart of New York City and had little to no access to nature as getting to Central Park was too difficult. She experimented and found that even having a household plant provided some form of relief by observing it. Her mindful activity was sketching that plant and progressed to using color to note the details. As I reminder, I already reviewed how physically grounding yourself helps to regulate electrical activity in the cells but walking barefoot is still a practice that I do to maintain my grounded state.

In closing without addressing myriad other physical symptoms that rear their ugly head in benzo hell, I would like to encourage you to review the references at the beginning of the chapter to validate your symptoms. It is so important to know that your pain and suffering is part of the process of healing. If you are still having a hard time accepting whatever your symptom is (breast enlargement and/or testicular shrinkage included) then google a schematic of the central nervous system and see that it extends and is shaped just like the human body. My experience with working with others in benzo hell is that the fear of what could be wrong with them is driving the anxiety that is in turn escalating the symptoms. Once they know and accept that these painful symptoms are signs of healing then they become more capable of dealing with them.

Chapter 10
Can't Fix the Mind before the Brain Is Fixed

I am honestly not sure who it was who first said "You can't fix the mind until the brain is fixed" as I read a ton by following health experts and doing my research. But I am here to tell you that this is true in benzo hell. If the tightening, pounding headache that reaches deep into your ears isn't proof enough that this is an injury that shouldn't be antagonized with more stress or stimulation of being institutionalized or subjected to talk therapy then consider this. What happens when people have a physical traumatic injury to the head? They usually lose consciousness and sometimes go into a coma. The loss of consciousness is initially due to the swelling of the brain but the coma follows so that the brain can heal.

We have a chemical brain injury that is going to take our protection from as much as possible to heal and these psychological symptoms are protecting it from more damage.

The last chapter identified this new term for this benzodiazepine-Induced Neurological Dysfunction (BIND) for what is happening because of prescribed long-term use of benzodiazepines. In addition to what I already documented about this term, BIND's definition also includes this statement. "These symptoms may begin while taking or tapering benzodiazepines, and can persist for weeks, months and even years after discontinuation." I want to assure you in this chapter that while your mental health may be compromised during benzo hell, you that you have not developed a psychological disorder like Schizophrenia or bipolar disorder. Read that again. Well-meaning family and friends seeing your altered state may try to convince you that there is something wrong with you now and that you need professional help or to go into in-patient treatment. They are not entirely wrong in that something is wrong with us in benzo hell but it is not a new psychological disorder that has manifested as a result of this injury. It is a symptom. If the symptom is life threatening or you feel that you may hurt another person, then please get help *with* this information. But what I have determined is that once we understand that our altered psychological state is temporary and due to the injury then we are much more capable of accepting the distress rather than reacting to or on it. Here is a list of symptoms that are categorized as Psychiatric from the BIC website.

Psychiatric: apathy, anxiety, delirium, depersonalization, depression, derealization, distortions or hallucinations, dysphoria (inability to feel pleasure or happiness), fear, hyperventilation, hyperreflexia ('jumpiness'), hypnologic, hallucinations, sleepwalking, lack of concentration, nightmares, obsessions, paranoia, phobias (hydrophobia, agoraphobia, monophobia, acrophobia, anthropophobia, and others), rapid mood changes, suicidal thoughts, and short-term memory impairment.

I read *Brain on Fire* in the early stages of my recovery stage when I was basically reading two paragraphs at a time and resting. My friend Amy brought it to where I was living in month six as she was listening to my symptoms and thought they sounded a lot like what was written by Susannah Cahalan. She experienced a terrible month-long episode of having an inflamed brain mostly like from a virus and is wonderful at detailing how she felt along with bringing excellent documented resources into her investigation of her symptoms. I highly recommended reading it just for those resources that she credits with her journalistic aptitude and skills (she is a journalist and editor). But the take-away here as I delve into the mental issues that we face is that our brain's neuroreceptors are not working correctly. The goal of recovery is to upregulate these neuroreceptors and not need to add more medication. Unless you had a pre-existing condition that you were treating before ever starting benzodiazepines, don't think you need more medication for your bizarre symptoms. Read on to find out these mental are just symptoms of healing.

Visting NYC in Benzo Hell

The colors were so intense that I thought there was an artificial light behind the whole scene even though it was daytime. What was I thinking doing this? It was November 2018 and my daughter and I were visiting her aunt in New York City. I could barely handle the traffic on Ocean Blvd in NH but here I was after a long bus ride arriving in Times Square. My daughter was a sophomore in high school and had plans to attend college there in the city and her aunt was gracious enough to host us as she lived in Brooklyn. My brain felt like it was shaking but there was no turning back. The first and foremost strategy that I used was acceptance of my limitations and asking for support even before I got there. I could not have made this without her aunt's help so I was completely honest and made sure she was up for taking the lead. She was and did a fabulous job staying with my daughter for her college tour while I waited on campus. They were close to begin with but by letting go of the active role of "being the mother" and allowing her aunt to be the primary caretaker; the trip ended up being a huge success even if I couldn't be a part of all the activities.

How I managed to survive that trip was that I had a safe place to rest (her aunt's apartment) and combination of coping skills that I want to share with you in hopes that you can do the best you can to remain calm and more importantly, try to avoid such chaotic situations. Keeping your brain protected includes your eyes as we have discussed being part of the brain so what I did was cover them as much as possible. I had started this "tenting" routine at my home where I would tuck a sheet around my bed posts creating a veil of protection in my little tent. I did that as soon as I got back to her apartment and although I was buzzing from head to toe; I immediately felt safer and was finally able to doze off. Another technique I was using consistently was applying lavender to my shirt so I could smell it or even cover my nose and inhale the scent deeply. I want you to know that I was in no way educated or even believing in essential oils before all this. Warning: Never apply an essential oil to your skin and always dilute it with another base oil.

Derealization

I had extreme derealization (DR) on that trip to NYC where everything I looked at seemed fake. It was like the buildings and scenery were made up for a movie set and I was trapped in a strange world. I had DR bad in acute and in waves since then so it was not a new symptom and had already been finding ways to cope with it. The coping strategy is to embrace it and not run from it. Huh? I am not kidding. When I was doing my research on this and remembered that I had DR in high school (I did not know the name for it then) when we (my twin and I) had smoked a pot laced with LSD. I had such a bad reaction to that back then that I never smoked pot again, but here I was experiencing the same phenomena, but this was a result of a prescribed medication. So not fair. This technique of embracing the strange surroundings can only take place if you have (radically) accepted the injury and these symptoms with it. My friend Steve who has brought many comical insights into this awful benzo hell would go to the grocery store knowing that as soon as the artificial lights hit him that he would experience DR. He would say "Okay here we go." and just let the surreal experience become an adventure as there was no way to control it. I was doing the same thing in this situation as we walked around, and the pavement looked like it was alive and people looked like mannequins.

OCD, Intrusive Thoughts, and Agoraphobia

Other mental symptoms that often develop in benzo hell including Obsessive-Compulsive Disorder (OCD), agoraphobia (fear of leaving a safe place like home), and the most bizarre intrusive thoughts that you could ever imagine. My experience with OCD was immediately validated when I watched Brain Paxton's video on his story and what he had been through. Please see Reference J on my website under Resources. He describes being so germophobic that all he thought about was how to stay clean and he did not have this issue one bit prior to his benzo withdrawals. Mine was even more bizarre. My son struggled with his weight since he started walking and went straight to running and jumping at eighteen months. He not only burned through calories quickly, but he had little appetite. We didn't know what to do with him and his low weight as his older sister ate anything and everything, and she preferred healthy food. He would wait until the meal was over and after hardly eating anything good would then ask for cereal or ice cream. He was eleven years old at this point and was slowly growing out of this but was still thin. My new obsession was his eating. It became all I thought about. I was in fear of him wasting away and it was far past the time when that would have happened. There was no explaining this OCD other than when I got hyped up over something else; I would insist that he eat enough or start planning his next meal. I was a complete mess, and it was affecting his relationship to food. There was not a single thing that I could do about this other than separate myself from him as much as possible and hope that I would normalize with healing. And I did.

Dark and scary intrusive thoughts are common in benzo hell. Jennifer Leigh is both a Licensed Psychologist and a benzo Recovery Coach. When asked in an interview with D.E. Foster on his Benzo Free podcast if there were any mental skills that helped during this acute benzo withdrawal period and she answered, "No". It is true. We have no way to fix our thoughts until our brain is fixed. In fact, trying to fix our thoughts are mutually exclusive to radical acceptance of having this brain injury and holding the belief that we can heal. Fixing our thoughts means that there is something wrong with them and while we are not processing things correctly, the thoughts are not symptoms of not a mental illness but of the neurological injury."

I can't tell you my most horrifying thoughts as it would be degrading and possibly cause for this book to be called psychotic, but know that whatever it is that you are thinking and it scares you so you can't stop thinking about it that it is a lie. I often wonder about the most violent crimes in our world and how benzodiazepines could be a source of evil with people either coming off of them or sedated on them. It is a truly scary. Even though intrusive thoughts are an uncontrollable part of benzo hell, it doesn't mean we can't be vigilant about not letting outside stress contribute to the intensity of them. I had learned about a technique of imagining an invisible box around you when dealing with the outside world and/or people that I was slowly able to use as I healed. This box is your shield from the life disruptors that aggravate your desired peaceful state. The goal is to keep the issue at hand from entering our invisible box and therefore keeping that space around you sacred for healing.

Agoraphobia is yet another unexplainable symptom that I had never experienced in my life until benzo hell. The best way to describe it is that there is an invisible elastic band that keeps you from moving from a safe place and the more you stretch it by trying to leave the secured area, the more it resists and pulls you back. I don't think I would have ever been able to even believe this condition unless I had experienced it. It was beyond dreadful. I would cautiously peer out the window from my house knowing that I loved the outdoors and wanted to be outside with my family but that was not possible without first healing and then slow exposure therapy.

My aunt helped me make small goals in overcoming this, and the key to success was redoing whatever I had done successfully the day before I moved onto the next goals. I am talking about first using the front steps and then eventually reaching my daughter's garden which was about 100 feet away over a week's worth of work. This fear of being away from my safe spot (which was primarily my bed in my room) dissipated and then would come back if I was pushing myself too much. The reason why Agoraphobia can return is your brain calling out the actions as being too stimulating and needing that safe environment to heal. I have helped many people with this symptom by explaining exactly that. The people who are most successful at overcoming Agoraphobia do so by moving the needle with small goals and not taking long trips when they experience a window.

Depersonalization

Depersonalization is a symptom of feeling that you are not who you are but living in your body that is not yours. Seems confusing? Well, if you have the feeling that your limbs aren't yours, you don't recognize the face in the mirror and you can't seem to remember the memories that go along with pictures then you have depersonalization. Some describe it as a tiny person in you operating your body, but you don't feel like you have the controls. I can only say that this is a symptom, and it goes away. A coping method for it that we use is called "fake it until you make it" but it just puts a band-aid on the situation until your brain heals. I would smile and greet my children knowing that I loved them and didn't want them to know I was not there, but as soon as I was alone, I would cry with fear. My best coping method and healing strategy for this is complete immersion in the present and when the symptom dissipates to be aware of this preferred state of being with gratitude. This rebuilds the neural pathways for that normal state of being.

Anhedonia Is Not Depression

There is little doubt that we have every reason to be depressed in benzo hell. I knew that my life was limited, and I had concerns about my future but I was not depressed. What I had, and many other attests to, is not feeling anything. While I am sure that anyone who has not been through benzo hell will say that is depression, benzo warriors who make it out of this recognize this state as anhedonia. I had only one client who could identify this state while having it and that was after explaining that Anhedonia is simply not being able to enjoy pleasure. Why I think it is important to identify what the feeling is and not confuse it with depression is because of what this state signifies. Anhedonia is buffering you from seeking pleasure while the nervous system is healing. That is the function that protects your healing in this journey. I am not saying that it is necessarily a good thing to not feel pleasure, but this explanation helps to accept this temporary state. At four years off now, I am full of feelings and quite often show my emotions without care of embarrassment due to the time period of feeling nothing.

Rage and Always Being Pissed Off

The need to explode and blame others is overwhelming when in benzo hell. It could appear to others that you are always searching for reasons to be mad. These symptoms are more of a state of being than an actual justified reaction that I would like to address with as much transparency as possible as I am still working through it. I was using Ativan as needed to deal with stressful family situations so that I never developed consistent ways of dealing with anger. When I was in tolerance on Klonopin I relied on the shorter and shorter periods of calm instead of dealing with the issues such that I ended up raging with built up resentment as the effects of the pill wore off. If anyone thinks that taking prescribed long-term benzodiazepines are making them a better person by allowing them to "roll with the circumstances" then they are surely going to find out the truth sooner or later. Permanent damage to relationships from raging is not only possible, but has happened for enough people in benzo hell that it is documented in The Ashton Manual that there are high rates of divorce. This rage needs to be checked by you even though your brain injury highly compromised your capacity to regulate such emotions.

All hell of fury let loose after my foolish rapid detox. I was like a rabid dog in both bark and bite if anything caused discomfort in my protected environment. I am still pulling out of this state of being highly agitated for so many years, but I have learned some things that I hope can help you in to get through benzo hell without anger making things worse for you and others. Once you recognize a difficult or stress situation is causing you to become agitated; excuse yourself or the person from your presence. This requires some forethought in that family member or friends need to be told that your volatility is not something you are able to control right now. I gave no excuses for being this way but when I shared that my temper was my way of protecting myself from more than I can handle, I saw compassion instead of people returning the hostility.

Gratitude

What I can attest to is that finding gratitude for anything and everything is an effective means of putting out the fires of rage. Gratitude means having a deep appreciation. This appreciation didn't come easy for me as my old self believed that I deserves anything good in my life because I earned it. Not a good way to live but it is the truth. I am going to share the story on what made me start embracing gratitude with a significant event in my life. I was deep in tolerance during my third year with fits of raging as my main way of being. It was the most difficult time of my life. Period. And I was doing the most difficult thing I had ever done. I had promptly resigned from my first year of teaching job at the middle school after years of getting ready for this career transition. I knew that I had to as by the end of the year I was fully dependent on Klonopin (even though I did not know it) and my mental and physical health was deteriorating rapidly.

I spent the next year going to doctor appointments and being in a semi-zombie state and lying in my bed getting little real rest. If you remember the reason, I was given the ultimatum to get off this medication, then you know how things were going at home. My son was getting into trouble with school and sports more and more, and my husband and I were constantly fighting about how to discipline him. Read that again. I was fighting with my husband, and my son was fighting with everyone else. It makes total sense now. But it got to the point when he was removed from public school and a decision was to be made about his future. He was already competing in SlopeStyle at a national level by age nine and the next step for him was to start training out West where the coaching and facilities would be available to him. We bought a condo at Copper Mountain, and it was decided that I would homeschool him as I was a certified teacher. My daughter was still in junior high when we started this schedule of me going out west to school and take care of Stone while my husband switched with me so that I could come home for a couple of weeks in the winter to be with my daughter. It was a rough year for a number of reasons as the ski team he was supposed to be on at Copper didn't come to fruition, and we had yet to find his coach who he would be with for the next five years. I tell you all this to say that I was in a bad situation as I could barely handle Stone on my own to begin with, but now, I was trying to get him to do school work as teaching him was out of the question due to the constant arguing.

I need to note here that there are many ways in which divine intervention happens in my story but here is another way. There were brothers out there who are accomplished skiers who also trained without a team. Even though they were older than Stone by a number of years, they took him under their wing and saved both him and I that year such that Stone progressed skiing and I at least had some time for myself.

But I was literally at the end of my rope. I was in Colorado with no help and desperate when one of Stone's previous coaches reached out to me at a critical time. I had dropped Stone off at the barn (called Woodward) and this coach had seen what must have looked like complete despair on my face and called me that night to ask me to write ten things that I was grateful for. Remember I am cognitively impaired, completely exhausted shuttling between Breckinridge and Keystone, and I felt like death with fatigue and aches. I said no. I was not going to take the energy to write anything down and would rather die than keep going. He heard that from my voice and insisted that I did it while he stayed on the phone. It was a long phone call, but I finally understood the power of gratitude when I completed my list and shared it with him.

His affirming and gentle nature was exactly what I needed as coercion to do would not have worked. When I looked at the list and realized what I was battling weren't things but thoughts in my head. He and I both didn't know what was messing me up was long-term prescribed use of benzodiazepines but that didn't matter as much as learning how by simply recognizing what we do have during a time when we feel like we would rather give up and die is life - saving. I encourage you to do the same as I continued this practice of writing and/or listing what I did have that was good when I was feeling like these symptoms were my life. It gets better I assure you but until that happens – please recognize what you have and be grateful. This practice of doing exactly that builds our resiliency to what we need to go through to get through benzo hell.

Monophobia

One symptom that I did not have hardly at all (maybe like brief instances a few times) was monophobia which is the fear of being alone. Many benzo warriors report that they feel this way to the point of having to have constant companionship with another human. It must feel equally as terrible as being agoraphobic and I can totally empathize. I had my dog with me constantly so that may be why I didn't suffer from this. But I can tell you that this symptom can be part of your identity if you don't work to become free of it just like agoraphobia.

I am writing this book to help those in the recovery stage, and this does not apply to acute when you are doing all that you can to just survive. But slowly and when ready, start the process of being alone by successfully doing just that. The fear will go away, and I bet it will diminish exponentially as my agoraphobia did as I built on the small gains at first and can now fly across the country. But after working with families who have members insisting that they sit and re-assure them that they are okay twenty-four, seven, or almost to the point of affecting that support person's health; monophobia needs to be actively addressed by moving the needles as part of the healing process. A person who relies on other people for their health needs will not fully heal from this as that is the definition of healing – being functional and independent to the best of their ability. I rely on others all the time, but I am not dependent on them for my health and happiness as you will be too. And there is no better feeling than that. I assure you.

Chapter 11
Social Reintegration

To the outside person not in benzo hell but having their lives impacted by this iatrogenic injury, there is nothing stranger to hear how much effort the person in benzo hell is going to have to take to re-enter society. It is not a choice to have been so emotionally and physically crippled that interacting with others has been all but impossible, yet it appears to be easy to make a decision to start being more social. It is not. The reason that I write about the other people and not the person in benzo hell is because it is usually the social pressures from the circle of friends or family that make the benzo warrior attempt re-enter society too soon. But with this guidance and my heartfelt claim of caution, I encourage everyone to understand that the social re-integration does feel like a rebirth into the world. It is not easy but delineating how and when to re-enter society after this grueling experience is to make sure that the reader puts this on the way back burner and not worry about it until they are ready.

Social Media Pitfalls

This benzo brain induced injury (another term used commonly in our community) is isolating enough for us to deal with but the constant reminders from social media that you are missing out on things; it can get even more difficult to deal with loneliness. It may seem that seeing others do normal things would bring hope for us but more than often these images bring jealousy and resentment due to the nature of our injury. However, if you choose to prioritize your health with radical acceptance of this injury (including screentime is not conducive to healing as we have reviewed) then the path that you are on getting through benzo hell takes precedence over any social media allurements. I now can see posts on Facebook and Instagram and be totally happy for the joy of others. You will too but it takes time and getting to this point is not going to be quicker with more exposure.

I was working with a mom who lives in an affluent area and has three active daughters between the ages of nine and fourteen years old. She had great difficultly in stopping the use of social media while she was in benzo hell. She felt like she had not only to keep up in appearances how great her kids were doing but also felt more pressure to do more for and with them to be able to post about it. It was a no-win situation until she embraced that self-care needed to be her priority if she was going to heal efficiently. What she saw as meaningless tasks to do to get the rest she needed while she healed turned into rewarding ways to affirm that she was healing. Again, that mindset of accepting the injury and protecting it from as much stimulation as possible is needed to see the importance of the work you are doing rather than feeling like you are missing out on life while you heal. I am not saying to cut yourself completely off from the world, but I am encouraging you to take your injury seriously enough to recognize that if seeing others enjoy their lives is causing more distress, then take a break from social media please.

Recognizing How Small Our World Has Become

A difficult revelation for me in acute was how small my world had become in tolerance. I had simply not noticed that I was no longer connected to a group of people and had lost my sense of wanting to belong to a community. Other benzo warriors have shared their sentiments of this happening to them as well in videos, books, and posts. It is difficult to correlate the recognition of this with the needed time in the recovery stage to be able to do anything about it. While all the other symptoms in Recovery mode are addressed by "moving the needle" in the right direction, I am going to highly suggest hitting the pause button on trying to do any conflict resolution during this time. It is simply not the time.

We discussed how to prepare for this journey in Chapter 2 with whether or not to tell family and friends what is going on but what I am referring to now is reaching out to people you have not been in contact with to start rebuilding your community. I was a bit fortunate in this regard in that I had all but cut off constant communication with my friends in tolerance so when acute hit, I was not MIA on anyone's radar. If I had to "keep up appearances" then it would have doubled my stress in dealing with the injury. That being said, I was not happy with myself when I realized how small of a social world I was living in when I came to my senses and am still working hard to rebuild my lost social life. I will explain why and please know that I am suggesting this as the most efficient way for you to heal.

Social Awkwardness and Fixations on Educating Others about Our Symptoms

We experience a glutamate storm as the excitatory neurons far exceed the calming GABA that allows us to regulate our reactions and behavior. Triggers for anything that upset us are going to be felt in an extremely increased way so over-reaction is almost par for the course. I had mentioned in Chapter 1 about how people with autism have a high level of glutamate in their system and that could contribute to how they behave in a bit strange way socially. I have always prided myself on being able to look people in the eye and not be nervous in large groups as I have been confident of who and what I was. That all changed with this injury in benzo hell. Not only was I afraid of everything but I was so awkward when trying to communicate (often stuttering and forgetting my thoughts) that I felt uncomfortable around anybody at all. I was not raging as much in recovery stage, but I was still on high alert and therefore was triggered by minor things which would cause me to lash out. I was also obsessed with my symptoms and what I was learning about this injury to the point that all I could talk about was this topic. Many others experience this almost like OCD fixation on their story of how they got this injury.

My brain wanted to constantly ruminate on how to fix the medical community when I could barely cook myself dinner. And then almost like a person who becomes a savant in an area of expertise while being mentally compromised as a whole, I was designing machines in my head for at-home compounding of benzodiazepine pills. My engineering background is in electro-mechanical automation, so I was thinking of obscure mechanisms using actuators and scales to automate pill cuts to the highest resolution possible in a repeatable manner. I was never particularly good at engineering in that I was an applications engineer sticking to sizing motors and parameterizing the drives so this type of thinking was just bizarre. I have heard of others who have had a past passion or career start to become fixated with the subject during this recovery stage as well. One client who was raised in the church but had not been involved wrote his own bible of sorts in his head combing everything he had learned with practical applications. Phew. That is heavy. But like other symptoms, we just need to ride this out and know there is a good reason why our thoughts become deep and complex – Our brains are healing.

That One Unexpected Friend

I instantly overwhelmed the few friends I tried to reconnect with and even saw myself as that needy person who talked too much about myself for others to be comfortable with. It was tough to be that person after being so at ease with myself prior to benzo hell that I would now make others feel comfortable. I had to back off. But then I was given a gift from heaven again (not being religious but I can't explain it any other way). My daughter had become close friends with a girl who just moved here during their freshman year and I was familiar with her family from growing up with them as a child with grandparents who lived near her grandparents. It was this girl's grandmother who saved me in many ways by accepting my injury and encouraging me to do things with her on almost a daily basis. We walked our dogs together, we gardened together, we talked and laughed, we shared recipes and cooked, we drove doing errands together, we did quilt projects together and she never once judged me for saying that I was either too tired or overwhelmed by a situation.

I know not everyone will find someone like that, but I can tell you that being open and curious enough to allow this lady (her name is Toppy) into my life immensely helped me to recover social skills just by being my friend. She knew I was highly compromised and didn't care as she wasn't comparing me to my old self but rather focused on what I could do and that was a complete relief for me. I am still good friends with her, but we no longer hang out daily and she is just fine with that as she wanted me to get better and become more independent. I encourage you to be open to new friendships during the recovery stage too as you never know how a person like this can also benefit from your company. At about two years into my recovery stage she sent me home with an article to read by Joanne Gaines on how broken pottery can be glued back together and made more beautiful (Kintsugi). Everyone should be as lucky as I was to have someone like Toppy in benzo hell.

Parallel Play

I would like to recommend some steps to take when re-entering life in the real world after being on benzodiazepines long term. Like a child who first learns to play by parallel play in that they play next to someone before they start interacting, short trips to do grocery shopping and/or other errands can be looked at as an opportunity to be part of society. Doing this with the goal of accomplishing a task and not finding reason to have deep conversation is important. I know you may think that I am being a bit over the top with this but trust me; I have good reasons for suggesting this tactic. I implemented this strategy for a good year after I got out of acute before opening myself up to be more social after an embarrassing trip to the hair salon in my first year. It was difficult enough to get to this appointment, but I made the mistake of explaining that I had been bed-ridden due to injury caused by long-term prescribed use of benzodiazepines and boy did I open a can of worms.

The hairdresser not only asked a ton of questions after confiding that she too took Xanax daily but also involved others in the salon and it was the most over-stimulating, triggering thing that I went through and not good for me and totally escalated my symptoms. Lights became overwhelming and my ears started screaming. Yes, I was glad to be making others aware of the dangers of benzos but with my hair in foils and the chemicals all but killing me, I felt like the minutes were hours with more and more questions. I finally had a great big panic attack and had to go outside (with foils and all) to do some high knee walking which helped calm me. I had my aunt on the cell phone advising me on how to diffuse the situation but I still suffered immensely for this as it took days for my CNS to go back to the baseline it was before the appointment. So, learn from me. It seems that we are almost programmed to talk about our injury so setting yourself up for this by engaging with others who you think need an explanation for your altered state is a recipe for disaster. I learned and can now either steer clear of the subject or dive right in depending on the situation without any repercussions to my nervous system.

Overwhelming Compassion for Others

As you develop your social skills and return to society there is going to be an everlasting change to your personality that will remain from getting through benzo hell. It is impossible to avoid. We empathize with people who are ill and/or need help in a way that can only be described as a sixth sense. I could have cared less about other people's mental state prior to this (unless they were family or close friends) and I certainly did not concern myself with other people's physical wellbeing. However, this is no longer the case for me and about 90 percent of benzo warriors who have been able to get to the other side of benzo hell. As a result, this community of benzo warriors are a tight bunch with real desire to help one another with few exceptions. Enough time must be given after the Recovery stage before we can be helpful as I learned from trying to coach others on my own too soon. I felt the need to validate any and all illness symptoms for everyone and anyone after feeling what it is like to be so sick for so long. My dedication to helping others was not helpful until I learned the proper skills (through my Health Coaching Certification). This may sound trivial to you but if you have ever discounted someone who said they were ill because they didn't look ill then you will understand that this is now the worst thing to do. No one wants to feel sick and miserable. I have felt the depths of hell and can't imagine being the person who would say (as I honestly did) – "oh, they are fine. It is all in their head." Never again will you look at a person who is sick with anything but compassion and understanding. It is just not possible.

DBT for Me

There is an invaluable class or set of tools called DBT (Dialectical Behavioral Therapy) that I have a particular insight into based on my experience. The first time I took a DBT class I was on Klonopin and in deep distress. I barely remember the course. But do recall being unable to connect to what other people were sharing as we were being taught how to balance emotion and logic. I was raging at the time and knew I needed help, but I didn't have the capacity to learn much of anything from this course. However, I did notice that people in that class were behaving differently by the end of the six-week class. For example: the man next to me had stopped being as argumentative and/or dismissive of the content. The tension within the group seems to dissipate as people interrupted less and were kinder to each other. I was out to lunch on Klonopin but did have the ability to recognize this transition in the class. The people who were changing were obviously practicing what they learned between classes, and I simply didn't have the capacity to do that while sedated.

When I was in the later stage of recovery, I found the workbook from that class and reviewed it with a whole new perspective. I was so impressed with what I was now able to understand that I signed up for the same DBT course again. It was a different instructor this time but the content remained the same with some obvious variations to the classroom management. I got so much out of the second DBT class that I started to be able to live like the person I wanted to become rather than being reactive all the time.

It is still a battle for me to remain calm and be peaceful when I sense that someone is being genuinely deceitful or unfair to me but my day-to-day life has much more positive energy dealing with people and situations. If you are finding that you may need help "normalizing" or even learning for the first time (if you were medicated at a young age) how to be rational and behave in an appropriate way when angered, then I highly suggest a DBT class when you are ready. We have many people in the community in various stages of benzo hell but you can always tell if a person is in acute by how easily they react with volatility to a suggestion or simple information that is new to them. These people are not ready for DBT but should know that there is a tool that will help them when they are ready.

David Powers Free Pamphlet for Family and Friends

David Powers is a benzo recovery health coach has created a free and helpful pamphlet called *Where Did Your Friend or Family go in Benzo Withdrawals? And How to Get Them Back*. The downloads listed on my Resources at my Website as Reference T. I am recommending this resource as it contains information that will help people understand what has been happening to you due to prescribed long-term use of benzodiazepines. It is a quick reference for those who have never heard of benzodiazepines as well as giving excellent tips on how to support you. He is working on a documentary as well so stay tuned.

Rebuilding Trust

Rebuilding trust with my children has been my priority these last two years. They were twelve and fifteen when I went into acute benzo withdrawals, but I had been in tolerance for over two years prior to that. I am still actively working on being able to follow through with any commitments that I make as well as just being present for them instead of hiding in my room. It was not the kind of childhood that I had hoped to provide them at all. I can't go back and fix it nor can I beat myself up with shame. It is a work in progress as I recognize the damage that I did to them while trying to make up for it. I can only say that whether your journey through benzo hell leaves scars on your family or not that we are so much more capable of love after getting through benzo hell and that will help heal them as well.

My Marriage

Why my husband honored his vows and stuck with me during benzo hell will never cease to amaze me. He married an energetic, fun person who loved outdoor activity and ended up with a bed-ridden wife who was unhappy. Even worse, I would have gladly left my marriage during the worst of benzo hell if I had been able to. I did not see any reason to stay in it as we were fighting most of the time and this caused further distress for our kids. In fact, I offered to remain in the apartment I rented after I left the home to find a calmer place to heal from this injury. My husband almost agreed. I was not forced to return but wanted to be part of this family again after I realized how utterly vacant I had been as a person.

I kept up the role of being a mother and wife but was unable to feel much of anything while on prescribed long-term benzodiazepines. This is not a fairy tale ending, but I have come to realize that the institution of my marriage that guaranteed our family's survival was and is far more important than I ever would have realized. My husband and I have made it through benzo hell and, in many ways, are closer than we would have ever been if this had not happened. It took grit and fortitude to pull out of a damaging way of communicating and become respectful of each other. I never claimed that I could do this by myself, but I wanted and tried to push him far away many times during the process of benzo hell. We had to forgive each other for a lot as well as learn that kindness is about being nice even when you don't feel like it. I can't tell you what to do if your marriage is suffering horribly, but please know that it is common for marriages to fail in benzo hell, so please learn from me being vulnerable here with you. If you have someone who is dedicated to the marriage and you can see that no life decisions are to be made during benzo hell for your own good, then try to ride it out until after the recovery stage to make any final decisions. I am glad that I did.

Chapter 12
Productivity/ Enlightenment

The purpose of calling this part of the journey enlightenment instead of "recovery" is to hint that there is much more to be gained from getting through benzo. This was my favorite chapter to write and hopefully your favorite chapter to read. It is literally all the answers I was searching the internet for in the darkest hours of benzo hell. Hope. The hope of getting through benzo hell so that I could have a normal life was all I asked for, but it has proved to be so much more than that. My windows and waves would cycle faster with less time at my baseline as the first indication of healing. I went through this process three times of getting these fast cycles before dramatic healing occurred as a result.

The first milestone for me was at about eight months. I had been living on my own for four months and it was time to start traveling to Colorado for my son's ski training and up until that point I was convinced that I would never be able to do this for him again. I thought I was disabled for life and that grocery store trips were about as much as I could handle. My baseline was such that I was able to exercise a bit and be present for family events, but my focus was still far from being able to plan anything beyond that.

My Clear Signs of Healing Upon Reflection – Rapid Cycling

Two weeks before the date that I was to switch with my husband who had brought my son out to Colorado to start training in November I was thrown into this rapid cycling of symptoms. This cycling included states when I was almost feeling like myself for a couple of hours and then was slammed with a wave that felt like acute. I was a wreck but had my aunt's calm guidance on how this happens when the brain is actively healing. Literally two days before the time when my husband had to return, and we would need to find boarding for my son I woke up with a feeling of clarity like I have never experienced before. It wasn't a window. It was my new baseline, and it was amazing. I knew that the trip out West would be taxing and prepared accordingly by taking every opportunity to rest and protect my senses.

I made it out there and spent my time enjoying the fresh air while getting back into the routine of being the primary care for my thirteen-year-old child. And here is the most tell-tale part of my new perspective of life; I didn't ski and wasn't mad about not being able to. Our condo is at Copper Mountain, and I am an avid skier. So much that I, in my most desperate and regretful acts of despair, told our then sixteen-year-old daughter (at the end of the summer) that if I couldn't ski next season that I was going to kill myself. Yes. I told her that. Why? I have no good reason other than they (husband, daughter, and son) were leaving to go on a white rafting trip in Maine and I was trapped at our ski house with such bad aches and fear that I thought I was literally in Hell. I tell you this because I want you to know that no matter how bad you feel in acute, you must believe that there will be an end to your suffering and life will be more meaningful without what you think you need to live. I know this is true with all my heart now but wish someone had told me or written that recovery isn't going to happen so that you get your old life back. The healing brings a better life.

Continued Progress and Life Returning but Wave Hit

I continued to feel better and better and even attempted to ski by March 2019 which meant that I took a few slow runs and that was it. There were a couple more trips back and forth to Colorado as my son was training with a team by this point and things were steadily improving with our family. I moved back home for good and was adjusting to having a limited life but learning more and more about ways to achieve optimal health. Then the dreaded twelve-month wave hit. It was devastating. The aches raged back, and my body shook. Unlike my eighteen-month wave, this wave hit without me doing something over the top but rather from me increasing my duty-cycle such that I was simply not resting enough. I had felt it coming but was so excited about being an active part of my family and possibly starting to live a more normal life that I avoided what I should have paid attention to. We develop this sense about our health after going through benzo hell that is difficult to explain other than there is a deep connection to how our bodies and brain are doing and whether there is an issue. This is not the constant body scanning followed by exhaustive searches on what could be wrong but an inner feeling of what our we need to maintain our well-being.

POTS

The twelve-month wave brought a new symptom as well as the deep fatigue and many other distresses. The new symptom was POTS. It is a condition where your heart rate rapidly increases when you stand or exert any energy that is not proportional to the amount of physical activity but drastically escalated. It is both horrendous and terrifying. Why would I be talking about another symptom of benzo hell in this section of the book that is supposed to be about the best part of the recovery? Because I was able to take what I learned from the first Recovery stage and apply it with confidence this time. The wave last about three months and essentially had me living isolated and alone all summer again. Even the inability to be in the sun returned with a vengeance.

Was I dreadfully upset and suicidal this time compared to last summer? Nope. Not at all. I regrouped using the mindful protocol and did what I had done to get through this acute wave the second time. I persevered in taking extremely good care for myself and then the fast cycling between windows and waves started again. It took about ten days of extreme ups and downs where I was feeling like I could do anything at times but know that I should not act like I am healed and then times of such anxiety and fear that I was in Hell again. And then – I emerged with a new higher baseline. This was in late summer/early August, and I can't tell you how grateful I was to be alive.

New Endeavors with More Meaning

It was then that I pursued this new career in Health coaching as I wanted to be part of the solution and felt that I had learned enough to help others. Getting my health coaching certificate was therapeutic as I interacted with others on similar paths of becoming healthier themselves and learning how to help others to become healthy. I attended a conference for the Health Institute in Texas that was the most eye-opening event for me as I met fifty to sixty people (at least) who heard my story and wanted to either learn more or get help. From me. I was now an expert on something that so many people were struggling with, and it felt great to help them by simply validating that long-term use of benzodiazepines were the cause for their ongoing ailments.

I hadn't "conquered" this injury from prescribed long-term use of benzodiazepines as my previous self would have liked to have given my personality. I had learned to accept it and be gentle with the healing process while doing the best I could to develop and maintain healthy lifestyle habits. But as you know if you read the chapter on Nutrition – Fuel to Heal, I was to have another horrendous acute wave at eighteen months from self-inflicted and family stress, so my recovery was far from complete. But I survived that in much of the same way, and by two years off, I was a functional, productive, and much happier person than I would have ever dreamed I could be.

Developing Your Resiliency

There is a resource that I would like to promote. It is a book by Rick Hanson called *Resilient*. While he does have programs available online, I am recommending this book during the recovery stage as it helped me immensely without over committing my available energy. It was a like a bible to me over the years, and I use his teachings to help others. The most important take-way from his book that applies to us in benzo hell is to "keep pruning the tree." A tree weathers all the seasons without being able to hide from the elements and even becomes dormant for protection in the winter. To get the tree to reclaim its vitality in the Spring, one may have to prune the dead growth so that it can concentrate on new growth. We must decide to do the same thing in the recovery stage after getting out of the acute stage when being dormant is the only way to survive. There is no way around, under or over benzo hell but only getting through it. Unfortunately, this is the truth and I hope I have not miscommunicated this in my book. What we need is to be resilient as we heal and to get through benzo hell. But that doesn't mean we stop actively doing what helps that. We cut off our dead growth and prune our bodies when we choose to prioritize our health over chasing the old life and giving away our energy to heal. As Rick says, "if the tree isn't blooming as expected then keep pruning the tree." This is resiliency, and it will get you through benzo hell.

Emerging with a New More Compassionate Personality

With the practice of gratitude in the recovery stage, I and many others become different people with compassionate personalities instead of being competitive about life. I lean into stories of triumph when there has been a struggle in a way that I would not have even considered before this. And what you will discover as you get through benzo hell is that the person who you became on prescribed long-term benzodiazepines wasn't you. Hobbies and interests flood back when the brain is ready to have such thoughts and ability for follow through. I have always loved doing home repair projects like painting and woodwork. I hadn't done any of that in years while on Klonopin and having this injury. I now am rediscovering that joy but still being careful about chemical fumes (which produce mild symptoms still). Your interests in what used to bring you pleasure are not gone. They are simply not accessible if you are in benzo hell. You will be you again. I promise. The hard part is that there isn't a set time frame so finding another person who was on the same dose for the exact amount of time is useless for comparison. What healing comes down to is you and your ability to accept the process without judgment of being unable to do everything you used to do while injured. That is the way you heal. I am reluctant to address those who haven't healed as there are a select few in our community but I would like to simply say that I believe we all have the capacity to heal. That does not mean everyone heals. You have to make that decision and follow through for yourself.

Being Productive: What does that mean now?

Being productive for me means something entirely different now. Before I thought that getting as much physically possible done was being productive. That is simply not true. I am doing all that is required of me and need little assistance but my primary goal each day is to enjoy my health. It is not a selfish quest but rather a choice that allows me to give even more of myself to others with being much more present with them rather than rushing around trying to fit everything in. I had read about being a "Bisy Backson" in the world of Pooh Bear but had not clearly understood the concept until this experience. For those who don't know about the Bisy Backson concept; it is a comical strife on the person who is always out doing something so that when their friends and neighbors stop by the sign misspelled by Rabbit reads Busy Back Soon. I was indeed a Bisy Backson prior to this injury and is partially why I ended up on benzodiazepines.

I no longer feel compelled to do nearly as much as I used to do but have not become lazy as a result. My efforts are more focused and I can balance the business, housework and family obligations with much more ease and enjoyment because of my new lifestyle. And this will be the best part for you to hear is that I have no baseline anxiety. Many people report that this unbelievable transformation occurs as a result of getting through benzo hell. I still get nervous and/or excited about some things but that tight dread in my chest and throat has left the building. I have had several small incidents over the last two years due to stressful circumstances (driving to NYC to both drop off my daughter and pick her up from college) but I know how to calm myself after and have been blessed with having friends from our community for support. Thank you, Steve, especially for this.

Becoming Again and Playing Golf Instead of Tennis

I would like to say that I am aging backward but I am simply experiencing a rapid return to what I should look and feel like at my age. The last two years have been truly amazing as I have been able to get my muscle mass back with regular workouts and have increased my physical stamina such that I am playing in a golf league. I skied a ton last winter and enjoyed traveling. We are venturing onto new family excursions with buying a boat and getting out on the ocean as I used to do when I was growing up. My dog is still by my side almost all the time and we walk every day either in the woods or on the beach. I wake up and don't feel dread. There is a welcomed urgency to get out of bed and start the day even though I still have to take this part of the day slow.

My executive function skills are returning, and I can finally help with higher level household tasks like dealing with health insurance and bills. While I continue to coach others in benzo hell for the time being, I am planning on returning to my education career goals in the future. I am writing this book to put the past behind me knowing that I am going to continue to heal from this iatrogenic injury that took years from my life. It can't be said or written enough, in my opinion, that there is a whole new life after benzo hell, and it is better than you would have ever expected. I am proof of where there is no evidence-based research on healing from this injury.

Perspective on Life Changes

The term may sound tacky but we become benzo warriors when we are getting through benzo hell. We do not become benzo worriers. A warrior has resilience when faced with hardship. A worrier crumbles with doubt in adverse conditions. There are still fleeting moments when a particular symptom returns or something new pops up that my old personality of trying to fight the symptoms returns. But being a benzo warrior means doing the opposite. I recognize the symptom as the iatrogenic injury from prescribed long-term use of benzodiazepines and accept that it will take time to pass and do what I can to facilitate that process. How is that being benzo warrior? It is having the inner strength to not chase the symptom due to worry which could impede recovery. That strength is what is keeping me healthy to this day and I am hoping that keeps you on this path through benzo hell instead of trying to find ways around, over or under it. A benzo warrior has the belief that going through benzo hell will heal them. And that belief is what ends up healing them.

Chapter 13
All the Reasons Why We Fail to Get Off of Benzos and Regain Our Health

This book is not a campaign to get off prescribed long-term benzodiazepines but rather a resource to aid you in getting through benzo hell. Therefore, I have saved the four most difficult symptoms to manage as they develop in tolerance, peak in acute when totally off the medication and the real work to heal from them begins in the recovery stage. These symptoms will most likely also be your reasons why you may choose to not come off this medication sooner or if at all. The fatigue, depression, anxiety and what you think is the quality of your life most likely will get worse before it gets better. Hold on now. Why would I encourage you to get off a medication that will cause worsening of these issues when you picked up this book hoping for a better, healthier life? The answer is that there is only one way through benzo hell to get to the other side where life is indeed better in ways that you may not even have imagined. Here are those four reasons for and help dealing with their symptoms so that you can get to the other side of benzo hell.

Fatigue and Spoon Theory

An intense game of playing sports or a long day taking care of small children can leave you feeling tired. I have also landscaped as full-time job, been in the field traveling for automation and felt what it is like being a classroom teacher who hardly gets any breaks in the day. But nothing I have experienced comes even close to comparing to the fatigue felt upon waking up in benzo hell. This is not even that heavy, weighted feeling of depression. It is the type of exhaustion when lifting your head up takes effort and a walk to the refrigerator feels like a monumental event. If you read about chronic fatigue syndrome while you are experiencing this dreadful symptom, it describes it perfectly. And we may in fact have CFS for a temporary period of time as part of this recovery. It is difficult to accept that our bodies could betray us like this, but it is happening for a reason. The energy in our cells comes from the mitochondria.

I noted the dreadful fatigue in tolerance when I was simply doing what I could in between laying down. That fatigue became 100 times worse in acute due to my foolish rapid detox. But even with a proper taper, you will most likely experience this period of having CFS and it is part of the healing process. Remember that we are regenerating neural pathways that have been inhibited and therefore lost due the prescribed long-term use of benzodiazepines. When we are finally free of the medication but have excess glutamate, our bodies are in overdrive constantly with the flight or fight syndrome. So how are we supposed to take the time to rest and heal in such a state? The fatigue is (or hypothesized) due to our cells needing that rest to store up energy in the mitochondria for healing. It is literally our bodies and brains preventing us from doing anything else as we heal. Therefore, we are forced to rest in this awful fatigue but accept the process knowing that it is part of recovery. Anyone who says that you need to walk around to generate energy or regain your physical stamina while in acute doesn't know what they are talking about. You will feel the energy return but not by pushing through this symptom.

Spoon Theory

I subscribed to the Spoon Theory after a good friend introduced me to it. It is about planning your day when you feel chronically ill so that the tasks are prioritized without draining your reserve energy. Please research this on your own but it is essentially assigning a spoon to an activity or task knowing that you have only limited amounts of spoons for the day. I literally had five to six spoons a day to use while in acute and they were used for bathing, dressing, filling my water bottles, going to the bathroom and eating. I am not kidding. I had to allot these tasks with segments of energy (spoons) to both pace myself and be okay with knowing that I had a limit that could not be exceeded. I don't use the spoon theory now but I was still using it in the later stage of recovery and would allot twenty to twenty-three spoons a day. And an important reminder here: this a nonlinear healing process so that the use of the spoons didn't increase on a weekly basis as sometimes I had less energy available regardless of what I had done the week before.

Depression and Suicidal Ideation

With all these symptoms and the suffering of going through benzo hell, it is no wonder that we also succumb to depression. Everyone in benzo hell gets sad and mad about this situation for sure. The depression has been described by one of my clients has wearing a dark veil that allows in no light. This type of depression doesn't just manifest out of circumstances but also hijacks our brains to make us believe that life isn't ever going to be worth living again. I had this to the nth degree in Tolerance as well. I called my sister-in-law one time and said that I was not able to handle this life anymore and that my family would be better off without me. That was a mistake. Both the call (as I suffered intentional humiliation instead of support) and that decision. It was a benzo Lie. I was severely depressed not because of my life circumstances but my inability to handle them as I was too sedated to even think pro-actively or even reasonably. I am no longer depressed and see that an attempt to exit my life would have been not only disastrous for my family but would have prevented me from finding the happiness and joy that I now have.

Also, no one would want to continue to live in the acute stage of benzo hell but what I am hoping that you understand from this is that it is a temporary (but sometimes long acting) part of the recovery. Those who chose to take their lives due to being in acute could not handle the suffering any longer. We had a beloved benzo warrior leave a suicide note after suffering for years in which she details how further medical interventions lead to more pain and prolonged her healing past the point of being able tolerate that suffering. You now know that there is a way to heal from it and it doesn't include more medications or rapid detoxes in a medical facility. Those interventions just add to the problem in the end.

There is a book that helped me to recognize that depression was causing me to think irrationally. It is called *Feeling Good* by David Burns. It has a couple of ways and resources to deal with depression that I found to be effective. It is a rather large book and I had difficulty comprehending much of what I was reading at first, but it made me realize that our thoughts when this severely depressed are not reality. In fact, these thoughts are so much different than the actual reality that we start fabricating reasons to believe those thoughts. He uses a patient who is healing from a heart surgery as an example. This patient is slowly making progress by doing laps of the hospital floor but when confronted with the truth of how much he has accomplished, he goes on to make up a story of how there was construction rerouting his route and therefore made it shorter for him to complete. That is depression talking and not reality. You will have reasons to be sad as you endure suffering in benzo hell but the deep, dark depression is just a symptom and that is all. This whole book will explain how much better it will be on the other side of benzo hell.

Higher Power

I have a belief that a higher power did carry me through the worst of this depression as I let it take control when I had given up. Again, I am not religious, but I did find that there was a higher power willing me to continue to live as others in benzo hell report sensing that they are not alone for the first time in their lives too. I wish I could explain how to directly facilitate this connection to a higher power but I can only encourage you to do what I did. I let go of my struggle to decide whether to end my life or not by giving control of that decision to this higher power. This option presented itself to me just as I was at the end of my rope – literally. I saved myself but I did by allowing that higher power to take over. I am much a believer now in what prayer and God (whatever you want to call that Higher Power) can help save us from this temporary depression.

I found this quote on Instagram from the Depression Project and want to use it here as it fits perfectly for what we are experiencing in benzo hell.

"It's not your life that is the problem. It's this chapter. Please hold on. There is a new chapter ahead and you'll be glad that you stayed for it."

Rebound Anxiety

Sheer desperation is what led to me ending up in the psychiatrist's office when I was having heart palpitations that scared the absolute crap out of me.

These heart palpitations that included missed beats, extreme pounding, and tachycardia (irregular heartbeat) that were the result of interdose withdrawal of Ativan. I had been to many other doctors to find out what was causing the increasing headaches and panic attacks but these heart issues put me over the edge. I made the appointment with the Psychiatrist after being told to by these doctors who could not find anything wrong. It wasn't that I was trying to avoid more head medication (at that point) but I honestly didn't know what was causing these symptoms. All I knew was that I was desperate to keep my new teaching career that I had worked so hard for, and these symptoms were jeopardizing that. In being as truthful as possible, it was a relief when she told me that I needed something "different than Ativan" and said that this new medication was something I could take daily, even twice a day. Had I known all that I know now that it was simply the same medication but stronger with a longer half-life and that she had doubled the dose of the benzodiazepine (which I didn't even know that word yet) then I would have run for the hills. I foolishly did no research into the medication as I trusted her completely. All I knew was that it was going to help me with a chemical imbalance in my brain. Let it be known that without a doubt the anxiety that you are feeling when using this medication is not going to be fixed by taking more of it. It just prolongs the misery with short periods of feeling calm.

Regular Anxiety Is Good for You

If you think I know a lot about benzodiazepines now, then let me assure you that I know even more about anxiety as a symptom of human nature and why it happens. Humans have anxiety for a reason. It is our indicator that something is wrong and change is required. Allowing anxiety to fester without action and then getting into a (what feels like) a life-or-death situation leads to panic attacks. Yes, panic attacks can be brought on by other health factors such as dehydration or overworked exhaustion but this is still within our control to prevent or deal with. The chemically enhanced anxiety that I was experienced while working all hours at that middle school without support or appreciation for my efforts was my body telling me that I was overexerting my efforts in the wrong area of my life during that period of time.

My family needed me with two young children at home and my heart was there. While I had a passion for teaching Math, my brain couldn't validate the stress I was putting on the family when we certainly didn't need the added income even if the health insurance was helpful. I had bit off way more than I could chew and that was why I took more Ativan and why I ended up on Klonopin. What I should have done with this anxiety is what I do every day when I feel some strain between my heart and my head which is to listen to it. I am living a life now that is in accordance with my beliefs and my efforts are concentrated on what matters to me. I still want to return to teaching middle school mathematics but that was not the right time for expelling so much energy in a dismissive environment. I have learned to use both nutrition and gentle exercise as a means to build my resiliency and have the capacity to recognize what is causing me stress without trying to just "suck it up" and deal. I use my coping skills to calm down and make necessary changes. But this was a long process to get here.

Anxiety Disorder Questioned

Before you ask if I believe there is such a thing as an anxiety disorder that needs medication for treatment, let me ask you this. Have you done everything that you can for your body to support it dealing with stress in natural ways and if so, is there a possibility that your anxiousness means that something is not right in your life and needs to be changed? If you answer "Yes" and then "No" to those sequential questions while not on medication, then I will then answer your question not as a medical expert but as your friend. Finding a real solution to your anxiety may start with some medical intervention (like medication) but finding peace that lasts is still going to be up to you. There is life and health coaches (not psychiatrists.) who can help you identify what is causing and what can help control your anxiety. I should have hired one with the training that I got from the Health Coach Institute as they would have asked the right questions and I would have gotten the help I needed. That help would have included been a significant change to my diet in slow moderate steps, making self-care a priority, being present instead of hiding from the obvious signs of overload and using the resources that I had to make the necessary changes in my career. Instead, I relied on a pill that gave me temporary relief from my anxiety but made everything worse in the long run.

EFT

In the worst of the chemically induced rebound anxiety of acute in benzo hell there was not much to do other than lean heavily on my husband and aunt who would tell me that I was going to be alright. I have never felt as anxious either before benzos or after benzo hell as I did when I initially detoxed off this medication. There will never be anything as difficult as dealing with this state of extreme anxiousness*. But as Gabe McCall on YouTube says, it is also called "paying the piper" as you (either unknowingly or knowingly) took this medication that alleviated all feelings of discomfort temporarily and now you are going to suffer the consequences. Sorry. That is the truth. But as soon as I made it out of acute, I remembered that I had learned about how to do EFT (Emotional Freedom Tapping) and it was a game changer. There are three statements, and I would often say "I am feeling panicked and I am going to be okay. This is withdrawals." With the meridian spots being lightly tapped in the sequence that is instructed and with complete and utter acceptance of the process which means not judging how foolish you might feel doing this; I would calm down and regain my capacity to think rationally. I would highly suggest learning about EFT online and be sure to understand that it is a practice so it may take a few attempts to become proficient.

*I wrote that sentence before the sudden death of my Mom and even that severely traumatic experience didn't produce the anxiety to the level of what I had in Acute withdrawals.

Memory and Warped Present

If you have been carefully following the timeline of my story through benzo hell, you may notice a fairly large gap from when I was taking Klonopin to deal with the repercussions of using Ativan as needed during my career change until I abruptly stopped taking benzodiazepines. I didn't get off benzodiazepines until three years later as I kept going to my psychiatrist and she kept refilling the prescription. I was indeed a mess in those years sedated on Klonopin but she just thought that was more of a reason to give me more medication rather than figuring out that I was getting worse from the medication. Recall that it was not my decision to finally get off this medication. It was my husband's hand that forced me when I insisted that my son go away to a residential program for his behavior issues. He initiated that I get off my anti-anxiety medication which he still didn't even know was a benzodiazepine. But what happened in that period of time between when I resigned from teaching until I did my foolish rapid detox? I remember that my plan was going to get serious about my physical and mental health while trying to do a better job raising my family.

Meanwhile, none of that happened. Klonopin became my only friend. I can't tell you what I did other than chase symptoms of feeling ill and becoming more physically disabled. I stopped playing competitive tennis, did less and less with my friends and I was home all day doing the bare minimum. I had always been an active parent either coaching or doing things with my kids for school and such, but I hardly even kept up with anything other than what I had to do during those years. My daughter and I took a trip to Rome during this time, and even though I am glad that we were able to take this trip together, I know that she was both the planner and the reason we were able to go (at fifteen years of age). She not only found our hotel after I had given up and was crying on the street but took herself on tours by herself when I needed to rest; yes, I let my daughter go without supervision in Italy as I was that incapacitated from the benzodiazepines.

I thought I was doing the best I could to take care of myself and that I would soon find the energy to get back to what I enjoyed. None of it came back. Taking 0.5 mg of Klonopin (clonazepam) twice a day became what I lived for and all that did was prove to me that I needed this medication to live. Benzodiazepines also bind to the GABA sites that cause amnesia and that is why it is used for medical procedures. It is not that I wasn't able to do much of anything in those years but even worse, I have very limited memory of those years as well. I will never get those years back, but I can say that whatever quality of life you are living now while taking benzos that it is not the best life you could be living. This is a warning though because no matter how hazy and difficult it is to remember things in tolerance, it gets worse in acute withdrawals but starts to get better in the recovery stage. I wish I could tell you that you get instant clarity as soon as the benzodiazepine clears your system but after long term use and/or multiple times on and off this medication that will not likely be the case.

It took time being in benzo hell before for me and many others to obtain the clarity of what your life was like on this medication. It may not be easy to read this and it may scare you but by knowing that memory issues are temporary and that you will regain your ability to remember things; I am hoping this information helps you. I told people that I had a brain injury when I would not be able to recall something or find my words or even worse remember their name. It was when I finally started going out in public that I realized how bad this symptom was as my phone number would elude me and I had to reset my debit pin too many times to even joke about it. Today I am clear of such issues and by paying attention to things now in greater detail; I can confidently state when I do forget something it is because it is less important to me than whatever I am currently concentrating on. In other words, I am sometimes forgetful but for the right reasons.

It Is Your Decision to Get off Benzodiazepines

It is your decision time if you are considering getting off prescribed long-term use of benzodiazepines. Nothing is going to make this easier for you other than knowing what to expect and possibly why it is happening. If you are already in benzo hell and were reconsidering getting off the medication (by up dosing or reinstating) then I hope you have the fortitude to stick to your decision to complete your taper. The only safe and recommended time to re-instate is if you are less than ten days off and are likely to experience seizures due either the dosage you were taking or abruptly stopping them. Many people who use the symptom based tapering protocol find that updosing worsens these four symptoms discussed in this chapter so be careful about doing that as well.

There are many videos of people in complete and utter hell on YouTube after abruptly stopping, re-instating and/or updosing. Some look like their health is going to prevent them from getting through benzo hell but I hope they survive and get to the other side. I have encouraged anyone considering this journey to prepare properly or as best as they can for feeling ill for some time. I wish I had the insight to tell you how long that will be, but, in my opinion, it does have a lot to do with how you treat yourself in the recovery stage. There are some who continue to work full time and that is far beyond what I could have ever done. These people still heal and some find the distraction of work to be good for their recovery. I just know what worked for me and others to heal as efficiently as possible. An invaluable resource from BenzoBuddies.org is this compilation of success stories that can be found on their forum which is listed as Reference I. Not only will these stories inspire you but they also give the real testament of how bad things can get before they get better.

Chapter 14

Summary of the Protocol to Heal as Efficiently as Possible from Prescribed Dependency of Benzodiazepines and How it Works

When reviewing the protocol that I have outlined on how to heal from long-term use of prescribed benzodiazepines, I want you to keep this in mind. There is no plan to deceive you to think that there is any other way around, over or under benzo hell. You have to go through it to get to the other side. My goal in writing this book is to promote a protocol that makes getting through benzo hell more efficient. My training in becoming a health coach started with understanding and applying that behaviors change beliefs and beliefs with practiced behaviors become identities. You are going to become a benzo warrior with the right mindset and your healing will be optimized by the acceptance and actions that you take. The radical acceptance of this injury that was discussed the beginning of the book can and will be the crucial start of getting through benzo hell.

Neuroplasticity and Self-Efficacy

When I was doing my Master's in STEM (Science, Technology, Engineering and Math) education in 2015 to 2016 I learned about neuroplasticity and the ability for our brains to learn based on beliefs. I would have never even considered that being successful at Math had anything to do with psychology until I had been exposed to this research. Jo Boaler is a Stanford professor who has revolutionized the Mathematics Education industry with her research and findings. She credits Carol Dweck with the theory of using the growth mindset to base her investigations on. I am not writing about Math in this book but what I want to share is astounding and made me a believer in Neuroplasticity and the capacity to learn and yes, heal. Healing from this chemically induced injury from prescribed long-term use of benzodiazepines is your body learning to regulate your parasympthetic and sympathetic nervous system naturally. The testament to having the ability to do something once that you believe that you can do it is called self-efficacy.

From Jo Boaler's conclusive findings, it was shown that students who believed that they could and would be successful at Math were able to learn and apply Math concepts much more readily and successfully than those who did not believe that they were good at Math. She has written books and articles showing self-efficacy promotes the brain to grow the connections that are needed for higher level math. The students' self-efficacy was built by psychological means of embracing mistakes as part of learning and having them see Math problems as ways to apply their critical thinking skills instead of just applying memorized formulas. The perseverance of being able to find the solution to a math problem was rewarded instead of the amount of time it took to complete the problem and find the correct answer. I am confiding to you that unless I saw the evidence-based research for this phenomenon that I would still believe that there are some people "good at math" and some people who are not. She has written books and articles on the subject and I was able to hear her speak in person at a convention in Massachusetts as part of my education.

Her findings are now being applied in the classroom across the country and we are confirming that once a student fully embraces their abilities to learn Math such that either old beliefs about themselves are abolished or they assume their identities as good math students that there is no real cap on their trajectory of learning. I applied this astounding research in my brief experience as a math teacher in two different classrooms with select students who had little to no motivation to learn as they thought they were terrible at Math. I, myself, witnessed them transform into being interested in Math and then quickly gain confidence as they caught up in the skills of applying Math. Obviously, I was excited about this new way of teaching using psychological conditioning before being prescribed long term benzodiazepines and am disappointed that I was unable to have my career change end so quickly. But now I am able to understand how important the belief system is for our recovery from this iatrogenic injury and am grateful for that.

Growth Versus Fixed Mindset

When we are in benzo hell and everything hurts and our minds tell us that this is going to last forever; our biggest challenge is to encourage our GABA neuroreceptors to upregulate and/or begin working again. Our neuroreceptors want to be able to regulate and balance out the excess glutamate so that we achieve homeostasis within our cells/bodies. It is going to be up to us to provide the calming conditions that allow us to turn off the sympathetic nervous system of flight or fight to restore the function of the parasympathetic to heal us. This takes more than just positive thinking. It takes the radical acceptance that we do have a real injury that needs to be protected and cared for until it is ready for a protocol that will optimize healing. To restore our ability to be calm when fear and overwhelming anxiety plague us daily takes us being proactive and "move the needle" with small adjustments in our lifestyle choices. We can't force these symptoms go away through sheer will but having the belief that we can heal will make this healing as efficient as possible.

As we go through benzo hell there will be doubts as this is part of the injury. Our brain is damaged and our bodies are compromised with toxicity and down-regulated neuroreceptors. The fixed mindset would have you believe that you will be this way forever and being chronically ill is your identity. Having the growth mindset that we can heal is how we get through benzo hell. We are not looking to find ways around it or over it through the suggestions in this book but instead are accepting that we can optimize healing so that we get through benzo hell as efficiently as possible. Being in an environment that protects your brain from overstimulation is going to allow the healing to happen. Using your imagery like what I use the trampled blades of grass growing vertically again is going to help accelerate the capacity to heal. Doing mindful activities followed by rest is going to retrain your brain to heal. Being careful not to overdo any activity in intensity and/or duration will keep your healing on track by not having a setback. And having gratitude that you know what is wrong and have the means to heal will carry you a long way in this healing journey.

We are a Community of Learners

Not everyone has an aunt trained in the field of Occupational Therapy and who has unconditional love for them as I did. But you do have this book. It is a resource that I have written to validate you and all these crazy symptoms so that you can get through benzo hell the best and most efficient way possible. My insights are from experience and learning from other benzo warriors. I want you to learn from what I have shared but also for you to remain curious about your healing and open to new ideas on how to accelerate the process (without trying anything risky that could potentially set you back). We are in this community together and the more we help one another the more we are a force to make changes. The ideal outcome from you reading this book will include making whatever efforts you can to help further the cause of find better and even more efficient ways of getting through benzo hell. The ultimate expectation would be that no one else suffers like we have by preventing any prescriptions for long-term use of benzodiazepines.

Call to Action: Informed Consent

Colorado is leading the states in their informed consent legislation bills. Massachusetts isn't far behind with Geraldine Burns leading the way. Informed consent would properly educate anyone who is considering taking a benzodiazepine prescription on how difficult it is to withdraw off this medication and that proper tapering is necessary to avoid long-term injury and/or even death. Talk about a person who has made a huge difference with her life after experiencing horrendous benzo withdrawals, Geraldine is considered the "matriarch" of our community. She has been on many podcasts and as well as her talking about her experience and she has helped countless others with direct support. Benzo Brains interviewed Geraldine Burns and that is Reference U under the Resources on my website.

Geraldine even spoke to Dr. Heather Ashton when she was still alive about this iatrogenic injury and the Ashton Manual. Garaldine's story is about being out on a benzodiazepine for no good reason (insomnia) and how much she suffered for years without the knowledge that we have now about this injury. Her latest podcast is listed as Reference V on my website. Her latest one, dated August 8, 2022 Episode 43 called Medical Prescribers to listen to your Patients, is a particularly important podcast as she lists (with the help of Benzo Brains) all the ridiculous reasons why people are put on benzodiazepines long term and some stories to go with them. Some of these reasons include ADHD, perimenopause, adverse reactions to anesthesia, adverse reaction to anti-depressant medications, alcohol withdrawals, back injuries, break-ups and divorce, death of a loved one, closed head injury, PTSD, Chrohn's disease, diverticulitis, ER visit, flu, Lyme disease, high blood pressure and the list goes on and on. None of these are good reason for prescribing the use of benzodiazepines long-term and the subsequent benzo hell that a person goes through after taking them for more than ten days can be and more often is far worse than the initial reason for prescribing them.

There was a black box warning on benzodiazepines cautioning against using the medication with opioids as this could lead to fatal respiration suppression, but I never saw that when I picked up my generic prescription for Klonopin. Nor did I see the warning about the negative effects from combining benzo with alcohol, but I think I figured out that one on my own and began using alcohol to heighten the medication's effect in tolerance (out of desperation). The FDA has recently updated this black box warning to say that the medication could be addictive when abused. This is not good enough in my opinion as the prescribed dependency comes from taking the therapeutic dose. And while there is progress on people becoming more aware of the epidemic use of prescribed benzos; there has also been such atrocities of patients being literally "cut-off" of their medication by doctors in fear of being called out over prescribing them haphazardly. Who knows how much violence and suicides results when people are put in this situation of having to provide for their family while in acute withdrawals. It is such a travesty of ironic proportions. Here is the bottom line from the FDA website on the Black Label and see if you can tell what is missing:

"Taking benzodiazepines for more than three or four weeks can put someone at risk for developing an addiction to them or developing a physical dependence without developing an addiction.7,8 The

FDA cautions that although benzodiazepines can be beneficial treatments, stopping them suddenly or reducing the dose too quickly can result in withdrawal symptoms that can be life-threatening. The agency warns patients to talk with their healthcare providers in order to develop a plan for safely and slowly tapering off a benzodiazepine."

Here is what is missing: Health care providers do not have the education or training to properly deprescribe so how is that helpful? Here is to hopefully having such knowledge so that someone in withdrawals doesn't enter the emergency room only to be put back on the same medication long term.

Jordan Peterson

Here I go off the deep end with my total and complete fury of how Jordan Peterson has handled his experience with his withdrawals from Klonopin. I missed the story of Stevie Nicks from Fleetwood Mac "entering the gates of Hell in her benzo withdrawals" as I noted in Chapter 1. But this renowned psychologist with basically the whole country watching as it was even reported on CNN barely escaped benzo hell. It was reported that he was flown to Russia to be put in a coma and he confirmed this when his daughter asked him to document the horrible symptoms that almost ended his life in a video. Jordan Peterson insidiously hints in this video that there is something that may have helped him or is now supporting his recovery but he has made no follow up information on what this is or how he is doing with remaining symptoms. He has the wealth, the influence, the time (obviously as he is still making videos on other topics) and the resources to help people in benzo hell and it appears that he has done nothing to advocate more research into what medically caused his injury and helped his symptoms. If he was able to be duped into taking such a dangerous medication, then it is no wonder we were set up for this tragedy of becoming dependent on prescribed benzodiazepines. Yet he continues to speak publicly on all sorts of mental health issues and on society norms about dating but has done nothing to help us find a real solution to the problem of prescribed long term benzodiazepines dependency.

Why am I crucifying him when other celebrities have had their battles with benzo and come full circle to tell their story? Mathew Perry doesn't even remember doing shows on Friends with his use of benzos but is transparent about that now. But here is the difference: the celebrities who had access to benzodiazepines didn't have an education like Jordan Peterson or the platform to teach others about it. We have lost countless people to benzo hell who all matter a great deal as well as many families being torn apart. But here is the real kicker: If one does an autopsy on the individual, they will most likely to be no benzos in the toxicology report as the suicide is to end the suffering and not due to an overdose of this medication. They usually end up overdosing on narcotics and then that person is blamed for being addicted to pain medication. The drug that killed them (the longterm use of the benzo) is not blamed or even recognized as the reason for their death.

I have been made aware of other celebrities who have ended their lives in the past five years who were dependent on benzodiazepines at one point in their lives and their identities would shock most of you. I am not able to share these names due to confidentiality issues but please know that it doesn't matter your fame, education level, income, or intelligence; we all go through benzo hell the same way. I was fortunate to have the economic means to be able to have resources like a wellness room built on our house for my sanctuary. I use this room now daily to escape the chaos and stress of family life but do so without hiding from life as I used to in bed all day. Your safe place is wherever you can find peace to heal. Money can't buy this mindful activity protocol alternating with rest. You need to implement those behavior changes for the brain to upregulate the damaged GABA receptors. Those celebrities and thousands of more common folks who have ended their lives over the torture of benzo hell didn't either know or believe that healing was possible, and Jordan Peterson is not helping these matters one little bit. Shame on him.

My Experience as a Benzo Recovery Health Coach: Not a Role Model but an Educator

I never wanted to become a role model for others in benzo hell. I invested my time in helping others when I saw that what my aunt was teaching me to do in this protocol was in fact helping. I never claimed to be fully recovered as I then pursued becoming a benzo recovery health coach as more of a career. What I was trying to do was provide the accountability aspect for other people to follow this to the protocol so that people would follow through and optimize their healing. While I have had much success in seeing people make it to the other side of benzo hell, it hasn't been a delightful venture into this realm of assisting others in benzo hell by any stretch of the imagination. I still get triggered a bit when talking to people about their tortuous symptoms and telling my part of the story to validate how they feel. I am finding that the people who are most receptive to my support are those who have not written their story yet. Meaning they are still accepting their injury but ready to learn more on what to do and what not to do. If I hear people say that they are "doomed for life" due to this circumstance or that, then I try to encourage them for a short period of time before letting them go as I don't have the time and energy to convince them of healing. I have even turned people away from my services when I find out that they have done the exact opposite of what I recommended to them only to come back and say they are confused why they are so bad off.

The truth is that once a person understands the iatrogenic injury in terms of needing to protect their health (especially in the recovery stage) as if they were in an infant; the person asking for help usually already knows what they have done to cause a setback or a wave. Time and time again I receive texts or IM messages from people who I have helped saying that they are in an awful wave and in that same text is the reason why. They know when they have done too much. Not all waves are predictable due to the nonlinear healing but certainly many occurrences of them are based on overdoing something too soon for what their nervous system can currently handle. By far the most difficult demographic to coach are males in their twenties due to their lifestyle choices and fierce attitudes of "fighting this injury" rather than accepting it. I made huge progress with a young man by sticking with him for ninety days every single day to make sure he stayed on track with everything in this book and it was a great success. But that type of support isn't sustainable for me as a person with many other interests, responsibilities, and commitments. So, I am left with the hope that this book can fill the void of not having an aunt like I did to guide me through benzo hell. It is my dream that this book becomes a resource for the people going through benzo hell as well as to be used to educate the medical community on how prescribed long-term benzodiazepine causes damage and fixes nothing.

References

References from my website
www.copperhealthcoach.com.

A. The Gold Standard of Medical Research: The
Ashton Manual (https://benzo.org.uk/manual/)
B. List of Benzo Withdrawal Symptoms A-Z (https://
www.benzo.org.uk/slistz.htm)
C. How Benzo Mimic Chronic Illnesses and What to
Do About it (https://www.benzoinfo.com/2018/04/28/
how-benzodiazepines-mimic-chronic-illness-and-
what-to-do-about-it)
D. Medications and Supplements To Avoid During
Cessation and after Withdrawal (https://www.
benzoinfo.com/medications-and-supplements/)

E. Why I avoided Doctors and Used the Internet to Get Off Benzos (https://www.benzoinfo.com/2018/11/13/benzo-withdrawal-why-i-ignored-medical-advice-and-listened-to-the-internet/)

F. Mad in America (https://www.madinamerica.com/2019/07/benzodiazepine-awareness-2019/)

G. Excellent Resource: The Alliance for Benzodiazepine Best Practices (https://benzoreform.org)

H. Video from Benzo Land of How a Benzo Competent Doctor would Handle a Benzo Injured Patient (https://www.youtube.com/watch?v=rNL20aYv96k)

I. Online Support Forum for Validating Symptoms (https://www.benzobuddies.org)

J. Brian Baxter Benzo Withdrawal Welcome to Hell FULL You Tube Video (https://www.youtube.com/watch?v=mNcPnnl6fdo)

K. DEA Drug Fact Sheet Benzodiazepines (https://www.dea.gov/sites/default/files/2020-06/Benzodiazepenes-2020_1.pdf)

L. A Word about Recovery – from Steven Wright, M.D. (https://benzoreform.org/a-word-about-recovery-by-steven-wright-md/)

M. How Chronic Administration of Benzodiazepines

leads to Unexplained Chronic Illness: A hypothesis (https://www.sciencedirect.com/science/article/abs/pii/S0306987718303645)

N. Neuroscience Basics: GABA and Glutamate Animation (https://www.youtube.com/watch?app=desktop&v=wP9QD-5FL5U)

O. Benzo Free Podcast by D. E. Foster – an invaluable resource for getting Through Benzo Hell (https://www.benzofree.org/features/benzofreepodcast)

P. One Year off Benzodiazepines: A Doctor's Journey – Dr. Christy Huff (https://www.benzoinfo.com/2020/04/20/one-year-off-benzodiazepines-a-doctors-journey/)

Q. Benzodiazepines Equivalencies and Why to Switch to Valium (https://www.benzowarrior.com/benzo-equivalencies)

R. Benzo Alliance BIND Symptoms (https://benzoreform.org/bzws-symptoms/)

S. DE Foster A New You: Life After Benzo WIthdrawals (Presentation Recorded Live at Benzo warrior) (https://www.youtube.com/watch?v=Nm3EwJFeRTA&t=1729s)

T. Download to How Benzodiazepines Stole Your Friend or Family Member – And How You Can Help Get Them Back. (https://www.powersbenzocoaching.

com/_files/ugd/
0cd875_f886f11f98534b72bbf05a225e0c6fc8.pdf)
U. Interview with Geraldine Burns by Benzo Brains
(https://www.youtube.com/watch?v=AvveKLgeBCQ)
V. Geraldine Burns Podcast – Benzodiazepine
Awareness with Geraldine Burns on Apple Podcasts
(https://podcasts.apple.com/us/podcast/
benzodiazepine-awareness-with-geraldine-burns/
id1358022441)

Blood Orange Night by Melissa Bond (My Book):
Melissa details her story through her own Benzo Hell
as her doctor prescribed 6 mg of Ativan.

The Benzodiazepine Information Coalition (BIC) has
an extremely useful website with amazing
contributors: www.BenzoInfo.com

These are helpful instructions on applying for
disability and other resources from their website.

Acknowledgments

Dr. Angela Lauria tells us that we "become the person who wrote the book". I have done that through using the Author Incubator process to finally complete my story about getting through benzo hell. If I was ever to learn something from this experience is that you do, indeed, need to trust the process for it to work. My own coaching efforts will be as frank and delineated as Angela's as she knew what was going to happen if I followed her lead even when I wanted to bail due to painful steps of reliving my wasted years. If we ask for professional help and then decide to continue to do what we are doing unsuccessfully then we are just wasting our time and their time. I will be forever grateful for the Author Incubator team for helping me move past my injury to become a published author who can help others getting through benzo hell.

About the Author

Jenny Karnacewicz, CHC, M.Ed, lives near the beach in Rye, New Hampshire, but can often be found skiing mountains in Colorado in the winter. She is a degreed engineer who worked in the electro-mechanical field of automation sizing and parameterizing electric motors and drives. Her accomplishments included being published in Design

World magazine on the hybrid microstepping when she was employed at ElectroCraft. After a period of being at home raising her two children, she went back to school to pursue her dream career of teaching middle school math. The story of how she became dependent on a prescribed medication by trusting her doctor's advice includes her losing her physical health and almost her family.

Jenny refers to the experience of first becoming tolerant on clonazepam, which is the generic version of Klonopin, and then coming off benzodiazepines, known as benzo hell for good reason. She and many others suffer horrible symptoms as a result of becoming physiologically dependent on this drug. But her particular story was made even much worse was the medically approved but very foolish rapid ten-day detox. It sent her into the type of internal suffering that is difficult to imagine but she gives the best account of it in this book possible. It is her goal to educate others on how to avoid her mistakes and share how she and others have healed by prioritizing their health.

The protocol that Jenny enlists to protect the nervous system while it recovers from being artificially sedated and then becomes over excited in withdrawals is based on intervals of mindful activity and active resting. Her aunt is an occupational therapist who had experience with brain injuries and knew that Jenny was going to survive what felt liked being near death, but she needed support to get there. Once Jenny became able to see progress from using her aunt's protocol, it became Jenny's quest to inform other benzo warriors of her success in recovering. But she needed to first learn how to properly coach people and with great effort and passion, she became a certified health coach to help others through benzo hell. This new education on developing and maintain healthy lifestyle habits propelled her coaching to writing this book to encourage anyone in Benzo Hell to take an active role in the healing process after the acute stage has passed. In fact, taking steps to regain health in the recovery stage has proven critical to prevent long term chronic illness from manifesting as she explains.

Jenny will always be part of the solution when it comes to healing from prescribed long-term use of benzodiazepines and is still actively researching ways to help people heal efficiently. Her efforts in helping individuals has been genuinely rewarding but she is ready to become more of advocate for public efforts to both reduce the prescribing of benzodiazepines and mainstreaming the treatment of withdrawals in main stream health care. Her ventures will include legal ramifications for abruptly stopping benzodiazepine prescriptions as well as making evidence-based research for this iatrogenic injury a priority. Her mission is just beginning as her health returns more each year while still battles quarterly flares of fatigue and joint pain. But she made it through benzo hell and is grateful for each and every day that she can be physically active and enjoy her family.

Other Books by Difference Press

Inner Genius Outer Guru: A Heart-Centered Entrepreneur's Guide to Unlimited Potential for Growth in Income and Freedom in Lifestyle without Burnout by Avadhi Dhruv

Longevity: Reinvent Yourself at Any Age by Maria L. Ellis, MBA

Leadership Parenting: Empower Your Child's Social Success by Mother Gopi Gita

The Empowered Yogi: Transcend the Chronic Pain and Anxiety Associated with Autoimmune Conditions by Maggie Heinzel-Neel

Embracing Equity: Best Practices for Developing and Keeping a Winning Multi-Racial Leadership Team by Janine Hill, Ph.D.

Weight Loss for High Achievers: Stop Self-Sabotage and Start Losing Weight by Karen King

Profitable Online Programs: A Brief Guide to Creating and Launching an Impactful Digital Course, Then Scaling Your Biz with Your Own Expert Book! by Dr. Angela E. Lauria

Kickstart Your Online Business: Create an Online Course and Start to Make Sales by Sigrun

Take Back Your Life: Find Hope and Freedom from Fibromyalgia Symptoms and Pain by Tami Stackelhouse

The $7-Trillion Shock Wave: 401K Investing Strategies with a Positive Impact in Our Shared Climate Future by Seann Stoner

Understanding the Profiles in Human Design: The Facilitator's Guide to Unleashing Potential by Robin Winn, MFT

Thank You

Thank you for reading my book, *Safely Taper off Benzodiazepines: A Protocol to Heal as Efficiently as Possible and Get Your Life Back*!

I would like to get to know you and determine if we can work together on your recovery from long-term prescribed use of benzodiazepines. But first, please understand that I am *not* a trained medical practitioner and therefore will not be providing medical advice. I am a benzo recovery health coach and coach based on what I have learned and applied in my own recovery as well as learning from others. Most of my suggestions and advice will come from finding out what works for you to move the needle toward healing. Thank you. Please visit www. CopperHealthCoach.com/FreeGift

What is your *why* for wanting to get off benzodiazepines?

Answer:

(T/F) If you are having terrible symptoms then the best course of action is to "push through" them.

Answer:

What is most important about recovery?

a. How much money you have

b. Returning to your old life

c. Having the growth mindset

d. Being okay with feeling ill forever

Answer:

The best way to "move the needle" is to

_____. (Fill in answer)

Please fill out:

Name:

Email:

Phone Number:

Medication History (dose and duration):

Anything else relevant (250 words or less):

Made in the USA
Las Vegas, NV
29 November 2023

81726633R00177